W9-CNF-251

This book is dedicated to the overworked attorneys and accountants of the Securities and Exchange Commission who were fighting on behalf of investors even when Congress was underfunding the agency. Without their selfless efforts, there would have been many more accounting frauds than the ones perpetrated in recent years, with losses even more staggering than what is described in the following pages.

AMERICA
ROBBED
BLIND

Greg Farrell

Wizard Academy Press
Buda, Texas

Printed in United States by BookMasters.

Permission to reproduce or transmit in any form or by any means, electronic or mechanical, including photocopying and recording, or by an information storage and retrieval system, must be obtained by writing to the publisher at the address below:

Wizard Academy Press
1760 FM 967
Buda, TX 78610
512.295.5700 voice, 512.295.5701 fax
www.WizardAcademyPress.com

Ordering Information
To order additional copies, contact your local bookstore, visit www.WizardAcademyPress.com, or call 1.800.425.4769 Quantity discounts are available.

ISBN 1-932226-36-2 hard cover

Library of Congress Cataloging-in-Publication Data

Farrell, Greg.
    America robbed blind: how corporate crooks fleeced american shareholders (and how congress failed to stop them) /Greg Farrell.
        p. cm.
        ISBN 1-932226-36-2

Credits
    Editor: Roy H. Williams
    Cover design/ text design/production: Sean Taylor
    Index: Brandi Williams

First printing: January 2005

— CONTENTS —

Introduction

Like a minister at a church revival, Sherron Watkins channeled a message that caused heads to nod up and down in agreement among her congregation. The only thing missing in this hotel function room off Times Square crammed with 100 fraud investigators was a spontaneous shout of "Amen!"

"I didn't recognize how corrupt the culture had become," she said, describing the painful days after Enron entered bankruptcy protection in December of 2001. The company had laid off 5,000 employees, abandoning them just before Christmas with no severance or benefits, while 75 senior executives gorged themselves on $55 million in "retention" bonuses.

Watkins had delivered this sermon on numerous occasions, yet it still came across spontaneously, as though her thoughts on what went wrong at Enron, and the problems ailing corporate America, were occurring to her in that moment. Ethical problems seep through a company gradually, she explained.

"It is not one small step in the wrong direction," she told the American Society of Certified Fraud Examiners. "It's walking down a slope that looks like an egg. At some point, you're over the edge."

Watkins, a no-nonsense blonde from Texas, was one of the few heroes to emerge from the scandalous fraud at Enron. In August of 2001, months before the investing public learned there was anything wrong with the company, she discovered the Houston energy giant's rotten secret: that it was using accounting tricks to fool investors.

In an anonymous letter to Enron chairman Ken Lay, she pointed out the problem and urged him to launch an outside investigation into the matter. Instead of following her advice, Lay resorted to a half-measure, asking lawyers who had already approved questionable business deals at Enron to conduct a limited review of Watkins' concerns. Not surprisingly, these lawyers found nothing wrong.

And so, instead of identifying the fraud internally and conducting a top-down house-cleaning, which might have preserved some credibility among investors and saved the company, Enron's managers blundered forward, unwilling to confront the truth. They maintained that the company's finances were healthy, despite growing signs that Enron's earnings were a sham.

In October of 2001, following a surprise announcement that the company had lost money for the quarter, reporters at the *Wall Street Journal* began to unravel the carefully wrapped package of fabrications that lay at the heart of Enron's overstated earnings. Once investors realized that most of the company's profits were bogus, they punished Enron mercilessly, driving its share price down to penny-stock territory and forcing the once mighty company into bankruptcy.

Enron's collapse vaporized $60 billion in shareholder value, and resulted in thousands of employees losing their jobs. Worse, it wiped out the life savings and retirement plans of an army of loyal employees and retirees who had placed their faith in Enron's promise that it would keep growing at a 15% clip.

Watkins watched this devastation helplessly. After a Congressional investigation discovered her warning letter to Lay and released it to the press, Watkins became a national hero, celebrated by *Time* magazine as one of three women of the year for 2002. She co-authored a book about Enron's collapse, and began a new career as a public speaker. She also launched her own consulting company, the purpose of which was to help corporations identify ethical problems and root them out before they festered into crises of Enron-like magnitude.

Her timing was perfect: in the wake of the Enron collapse and the subsequent exposure of a massive accounting fraud at WorldCom, Congress passed the Sarbanes-Oxley Act. This harsh new law, approved with record speed in the summer of 2002, was designed to close the loopholes that corporate criminals exploited to rob American investors.

Nearly every Senator and member of the House of Representatives bragged to constituents that he or she supported the new law. These lawmakers expressed outrage at each accounting blow-up. But few dared to admit the truth: the root causes of fraud at Enron, WorldCom, Tyco, and HealthSouth sprouted from seeds sown by Congress.

In all, fraudulent accounting practices at some of the country's most respected corporations destroyed an estimated $500 billion worth of investor funds during the recent era of corporate scandals, hurting almost every one of the 95 million Americans who own stock directly or through mutual funds. In all, the accounting frauds scared investors into removing $7 trillion from the U.S. stock markets. How did this happen? Congress never passed a law saying it was okay for companies to lie about their earnings. The nation's biggest auditing firms never openly endorsed a program to allow their clients to deceive investors.

And yet, in the late 1990s, business leaders, auditors and lawmakers turned a blind eye as a cancerous growth took hold among the nation's corporate elite. Publicly traded companies glossed over unpleasant financial realities and used accounting trickery to hit their quarterly earnings targets. A booming economy disguised financial weakness across the business landscape. Congress took no notice of the decline in accounting standards, since a healthy economy helped lawmakers get reelected. Auditing firms, instead of acting like watchdogs, boosted their revenues by morphing into advisers and consultants to their clients. Business leaders, who were paid in stock options, became fabulously wealthy folk heroes, their images plastered on the covers of magazines and the finance pages of newspapers.

Because things were going so well--for lawmakers, auditors and business leaders--no one wanted to rock the boat. The stock market was going up in the 1990s, after all, so even the Main Street investor was getting wealthy off the miracle economy. But when the Internet bubble burst in 2000, all the problems that had been ignored by Congress, patched over by accounting firms and denied by business leaders exploded into view.

These problems led to the exposure of a massive accounting fraud perpetrated on the public. These corporate meltdowns shook investor confidence in Wall Street and scared Americans out of putting their money in stocks. Only then did lawmakers see that their blind efforts to promote free enterprise and business growth had transformed the stock market into a casino where the roulette wheel was fixed.

This book is an attempt to explain what happened, to explore the root causes of these frauds. It is written not for the purpose of exposing new details about what happened at Enron, WorldCom and other companies, but to provide an overview of how the public got ripped off in these and other cases. Its goal is to give the average investor a greater understanding of how a bunch of greedy people--Wall Street investment bankers, auditors, corporate executives and their lawyers--defrauded the public on a scale not seen since the savings and loan crisis a generation ago.

Like that earlier crisis, this one was aided and abetted by the United States Congress. By passing a law that rewarded companies for paying their top executives in stock options, and by stripping the Securities and Exchange Commission of the resources necessary to police the stock markets, Congress allowed this $500 billion accounting scam to happen. The passage of the Sarbanes Oxley Act in 2002 should have changed things, but by 2004, observers like Sherron Watkins realized that the law would only be as good as the people it was intended to rein in.

After her speech to the American Society of Certified Fraud Examiners, Watkins and I shared a cab from Times Square to Central Park. She had another appearance that day in which she would barnstorm on behalf of corporate governance. But on this sunny April afternoon, as tourists and shoppers teemed on the streets of midtown Manhattan, she talked about how difficult it was to change executive behavior. The Sarbanes-Oxley Act was supposed to clean up corporate America, but from what she could tell, it only had the effect of forcing lawyers and accountants to jump through a few extra hoops. Congress could change the rules by which public companies filed their earnings statements with the SEC, but it couldn't change the attitudes of the executives responsible for those statements.

"There's a big group of companies that want to continue their behavior," she said. "They're not used to change. They want to stay the same." In other words, if we're not careful, it could happen again.

Chapter One

Executive Compensation

The day after Christmas, 2001, Harlan Waksal called his brother Sam with some bad news about their company, ImClone, and its cancer-fighting drug, Erbitux. After months of review, the U.S. Food & Drug Administration was going to deny their company's request for approval to market the new drug to the public. The brothers had spent the last few years of their lives working doggedly to develop and promote the drug, which promised relief to millions of Americans suffering from cancer. But when Sam Waksal heard about the FDA decision, the last thing on his mind was the suffering of cancer patients. All he could think about was his own bank account and how the negative FDA decision could wipe him out.

Waksal, the mercurial son of Holocaust survivors, had climbed his way to the top of New York society by combining the scientific promise of his medical company's products with his love of the glamorous life. He dropped huge sums of money on lavish parties and befriended stars such as Mick Jagger, but there was substance beneath the style: some medical experts believed ImClone's new drug could be an effective tool in the fight against cancer.

But the negative FDA decision threatened to shatter Sam Waksal's life. Most of his wealth was tied up in shares of his publicly traded company, ImClone. Once the FDA announcement was made public, which would probably happen within days, the price of ImClone's stock would plummet and with it, Waksal's net worth. Worse, Waksal had used his stock holdings in ImClone as collateral for a series of loans which allowed him to live like a prince among the jet-setters who divided their time between Manhattan, the exclusive Hamptons and a series of exotic vacation spots around the globe. The FDA decision would pull the plug on Waksal's princely lifestyle.

Faced with a financial collapse, Waksal reacted instinctively, breaking the law that serves as the foundation of the nation's capital markets. He tried to sell a big stake of his ImClone stock immediately, before news of the FDA decision was disseminated to the public, and ImClone's shareholders.

Following the crash of the stock market in 1929, Congress passed the landmark securities laws of 1933 and 1934. The crash had been caused partly by unscrupulous promoters peddling ever larger amounts of overvalued stock to investors, and selling out before the public learned the truth about the companies they owned. The Securities Act of 1933 made it illegal for officers of publicly traded companies to cash in on inside information. The law is the bedrock upon which today's stock market was built and the Securities and Exchange Commission, established by the Securities and Exchange Act of 1934, enforces it aggressively.

But on the evening of Dec. 26, 2001, Waksal wasn't thinking of the SEC and wasn't concerned about his fiduciary duties to ImClone's shareholders. All he could concentrate on was getting his money out of ImClone before the public got wind of what was happening. He placed a series of frantic phone calls to his father and daughter, telling them to sell their stakes in the company the first thing the following morning. Then, on the morning of Dec. 27, he tried to sell a chunk of his shares housed in his account at Merrill Lynch. But a young broker's assistant named Douglas Faneuil said he would need written approval from ImClone's top lawyer before he could allow Waksal's insider trade to go through.

Getting desperate, Waksal tried to get his Merrill Lynch ImClone shares transferred to his daughter so that she could sell them. Again, the request was refused. When Faneuil's boss, a Merrill Lynch broker named Peter Bacanovic, learned that Sam Waksal was trying to sell stock, he called Martha Stewart, his most important client, and left a message, warning her that ImClone stock "was starting to trade downwards." Later that day, Stewart sold her 3,928 shares in the company, for nearly $229,000.

On Dec. 28, after the 4 p.m. close of the stock markets, the FDA made its announcement regarding Erbitux. The stock had slid from $61 to $55 on Dec. 27 and 28th. On the next trading day, Monday, Dec. 31, it began to plummet downwards as investors realized that the company's wonder drug had failed to pass muster with the FDA. The stock price dropped 16% that day to close at $47. Over the next few months, the price dropped below $10 per share.

Whenever a momentous announcement affects the price of a stock, regulators take a close look at who was buying and selling in the days leading up to that announcement. In the case of ImClone and the FDA decision, it didn't take long for SEC officials to learn that Waksal's father and daughter both sold substantial amounts of ImClone shares the day before the FDA news.

In interviews with the SEC, Waksal lied about his conversations with family members and denied he was involved in any insider trading activity. But armed with cell phone records indicating calls between Waksal and his father and daughter on Dec. 26, FBI agents arrested Waksal in June of 2002. Prosecutors indicted him on insider trading charges, as well as obstruction of justice (for lying to investigators) and a separate count of bank fraud.

The SEC filed civil charges against Waksal, including one which demonstrated how little Waksal cared for his own shareholders. The SEC discovered that on the same day he was trying to unload his own ImClone shares, Waksal bought a series of "put" options on his own stock through a Swiss intermediary. In other words, Waksal placed bets against ImClone stock, and the more that ImClone's investors suffered when ImClone's price went into freefall, the bigger Waksal's score would be.

The jet-setting scientist eventually pleaded guilty to many of the charges he faced. In July of 2003 he arrived at the Schuylkill Federal Correctional Institution in Pennsylvania to begin his stretch of 87 months of incarceration. Reasonable people might wonder why Waksal would do something so stupid as to try to unload his stock just days before the FDA announcement. It's like trying to rob a bank without wearing any disguises: the security guards identify you on videotape in no time. But where huge sums of money are involved, even the brightest, most gifted scientist can be reduced to a greedy, impulsive child getting caught with his hand in the cookie jar.

From salaries to stock options

Waksal was not a stock swindler trying to fool the investing public or a con artist running a ponzi scheme. He was the CEO of a legitimate company who got paid primarily in stock and stock options. But it was that stock compensation that drove him to break insider trading laws. If Waksal's salary and bonuses had been paid entirely in cash, he wouldn't have had the same motivation to fleece his own investors on Dec. 27, 2001. If Waksal had been paid entirely in cash, the FDA ruling would have been a professional setback, but not a ruinous financial calamity for him.

The reason that ImClone's board of directors paid Waksal in stock options, on top of a healthy base salary, is because of a revolution in the way top managers have been compensated over the past 25 years. A quarter century ago, most top executives of publicly traded companies were paid a hefty salary. Some also received stock awards, especially if their companies achieved certain growth targets. But by and large, executives received paychecks to manage companies for the true owners, the stockholders.

Over the past two decades, executive compensation has changed dramatically. A series of obscure government rulings and changes in law, as well as the boom in technology, conspired to transform executive compensation from the salaries that most people receive into generous grants of shares in the company's stock. The short-term reasoning behind the shift was logical: if the CEO is paid primarily in stock, rather than a salary and bonus, he or she will work much harder to build the business.

But in the wake of accounting frauds at Enron, WorldCom and other companies, it has become obvious that managers whose compensation depends on their company's stock price at the end of each quarter have enormous incentives to make sure they report positive earnings each quarter, whether or not those earnings are real. The top executives at Enron and WorldCom claim they never explicitly *ordered* their subordinates to falsify numbers on their earnings statements, but they created a climate where their subordinates were driven to commit fraud in order for those companies to report consistent earnings growth every quarter.

Executive compensation goes Hollywood

Business fads come and go, sometimes in the course of months. But revolutionary ideas that change the way business is conducted evolve over a period of years. Their emergence is so gradual that by the time these ideas take over, they no longer seem revolutionary, but appear to be natural occurrences.

One such idea that flourished in the 1990s was the concept of aligning management's interests with those of shareholders. In the early 1980s, corporate raiders like Ronald Perelman, T. Boone Pickens and Carl Icahn launched hostile bids for venerable U.S. companies. The corporate raiders, saying they represented the interests of shareholders, argued that the managers of a particular company had grown lazy and complacent. As a result, they--the shareholders--suffered, because the company's stock price lagged.

In a successful raid, a well-financed shareholder--backed by mountains of loans--offers to buy a majority stake of the company's shares at a price much higher than where the shares are currently trading. After acquiring majority control, the raider takes over, boots out the under-performing managers and installs a new set of managers who have put up their own money for a stake in the company. If the new managers turn the business around, they become wildly rich.

In the 1980s, hostile takeovers led by corporate raiders were rare, but highly publicized. Newspapers across the country covered each raid like the business version of a sporting contest. Gradually, the idea that managers should have a stake in the companies they run took root in the public mind.

This idea used to be confined to the nation's business schools. In 1987, with the release of the movie *Wall Street*, it became part of the popular culture. The movie stars Michael Douglas as a fictitious character named Gordon Gekko. In the film's central scene, Douglas' character, who is modeled on the corporate raiders of the era, delivers an impassioned speech to shareholders of an embattled corporation he wants to take over. He declares that "Greed is good," and accuses the company's managers of protecting their cushy jobs instead of working for the interests of shareholders.

In the film, Douglas' character is a corrupt cheater who breaks the law. Ultimately, he pays for his misdeeds. But in corporate America, the concept of rewarding managers by giving them a stake in the companies they run was just beginning to take hold.

Easing of restrictions

SEC rules forbid company "insiders," including top executives and directors, from selling stock in their companies less than six months after they purchased the shares. Therefore, before 1991, if insiders wanted to exercise stock options, they were required to purchase the shares, then wait six months to sell the underlying stock. Because of these complications, most managers and directors didn't exercise their stock options until after they had stepped down from their positions.

In 1991, the SEC changed all that, adopting a new rule which changed the definition of what constituted a purchase of stock by company insiders. Up until then, the SEC maintained that an insider didn't buy the stock until he or she paid to exercise the options. But the new rule allowed insiders to date the "purchase" of their stock from the moment the options were originally granted by the company's board of directors, not the time at which the insiders decided to exercise those options.

The change suddenly made it easier for officers and directors to benefit from a surging share price in their company's stock: they could cash in options immediately, instead of having to wait six months. And, as insiders, they would be in a better position to judge whether the company's performance (and share price) would be improve or decline in the immediate future.

In January of 1992, just after the new SEC rule went into effect, the first President Bush took a fact-finding trip to Asia. With him were several top automotive executives from Detroit. On the trip, reporters questioned the salary levels of U.S. auto executives such as Chrysler CEO Lee Iacocca compared to their Japanese rivals. Iacocca and his peers in Detroit were paid millions of dollars per year. By contrast, top Japanese auto executives--whose companies were performing better than the U.S. automakers--were paid hundreds of thousands of dollars.

Democrats in Congress tried to limit what they perceived as runaway executive salaries. Up until then, corporations could deduct the full amount of their top executives' salaries on their tax returns. So Congress passed a law penalizing corporations that paid their executives more than $1 million per year by prohibiting them from deducting any compensation that exceeded that number. President Bush vetoed the bill.

A year later, President Bill Clinton signed a similar bill into law. The bill included Section 162 (m) of the Internal Revenue code, limiting the tax deductibility of every dollar paid over $1 million to top executives. But, as often happens with laws aimed at stopping one type of behavior, the intended targets of the legislation soon figured out a way around the $1 million salary cap.

The new law did not limit the deductibility of incentive-based compensation, so a board of directors that paid its CEO on the basis of performance could get around the $1 million limit. Stock options became the answer. Companies granted their CEOs huge numbers of stock options and deducted that compensation from their annual tax bills. The stage was thus set for a remarkable transformation in the way CEOs got paid for the rest of the 1990s. Over the next eight years, during a boom economy in which stock prices soared, more and more companies embraced stock options as a way to reward their top executives.

Unaccountable

Only one cloud remained on the horizon, and it was located in Norwalk, Conn., home of the Financial Accounting Standards Board. This board, known as FASB, is an independent panel that draws up the rules that accountants must follow when

23

administering their audits. By 1993, the FASB had noticed that one particular accounting convention was being abused to the point where it distorted corporate earnings statements.

What the board wanted to fix was how companies accounted for stock options awarded to management. The problem, according to FASB, was that the cost of those stock options never appeared on a company's income statement. And so a corporation could pay the equivalent of hundreds of millions of dollars in salaries, and as long as that compensation was awarded in the form of stock options, it would not show up as a cost. In this way, thousands of U.S. businesses inflated their earnings statements without breaking any rules.

To puncture this inflation of earnings, the FASB proposed a new rule: that all stock options awarded to managers and employees be counted as salary expense and deducted from operating profits. Corporate America reacted with outrage, promising to fight FASB at every turn. In particular, the technology community in Silicon Valley objected to the change in accounting. More than any other sector of the business community, small high-tech start-up companies benefited from the accounting rules that did not deduct grants of stock options as salary expenses.

It was a long-standing tradition in Silicon Valley for small companies to pay their key employees modest salaries, but motivate them with large grants of stock options. If these small companies had to deduct the value of those options from their earnings statements, many would appear to be money-losing operations, instead of growth companies. And if these companies appeared to be losing money, investors would not bid up their stock prices, leaving the employees with stock options that weren't worth much money.

Even after the disastrous bankruptcies at Enron and WorldCom, when some business leaders recommended that stock options be expensed, some of Silicon Valley's most respected entrepreneurs, including former Intel CEO Andy Grove, continued to support the old way, which effectively hid salary costs from investors.

In 1993, SEC chairman Arthur Levitt backed the FASB's attempt to change the rules. But he ran into opposition on Capitol Hill, led not by free-market Republicans but by a Democratic senator from Connecticut, Joe Lieberman. Lieberman, keen to show that the Democratic party could be pro-business, introduced a Senate resolution condemning the FASB proposal, warning that it would have "grave conse- quences for America's entrepreneurs." Lieberman's resolution passed by the lopsided margin of 88-9. Sensing that he was fighting a losing battle on behalf of FASB, Levitt urged the accounting standards panel to back off on its controversial rule change. Following the defeat of the FASB proposal, the use of stock options as compensation skyrocketed. By 2001, it was esti- mated that 80% of all management compensation came in the form of stock options.

As a result, many public companies were able to exaggerate their earnings. According to research by the Federal Reserve, in the period from 1995 to 2000, earnings growth for compa- nies in the Standard & Poor's 500 index would have been 9.4% if those companies were forced to expense their stock options. By not expensing those options, the companies reported earn- ings growth of 12%. According to a Merrill Lynch study, the expensing of stock options would have reduce earnings in the high tech sector by approximately 70%.

In his book, *Take on the Street*, Levitt described how the option expensing rule distorted earnings at Cisco Systems. The company reported a $1 billion loss in 2001. But if it had been forced to expense the stock options that it granted that year, Cisco's loss would have swelled to $2.7 billion.

Boards of directors justified the generous stock packages they conferred on their top executives by saying they aligned management's interests with those of shareholders. But that's not exactly true. In most cases, managers who failed to deliver results still got their salaries, even if the share price of their companies never appreciated. And owing to the technology boom of the 1990s, coupled with the rise of the Internet, the stock prices of entire sectors rose. Mediocre managers who happened to be heading up companies in "hot" sectors, like telecom, often saw their share prices rise.

Thus, by 1994, all of the mechanisms were in place to reward managers for jacking up their stock price in the near term, with no regard to the long-term health of the companies they led.

CEO pay versus the average wage

The famous financier J.P. Morgan once said that the proper salary for a CEO should be approximately 20 times bigger than that of the average worker. By the early 1980s, CEOs were making about 42 times the salary of the average worker. In 1990, average CEO pay in the U.S. was 85 times bigger than the average employee's salary. As stock options became the dominant form of compensation for top executives over the last decade, CEO salaries skyrocketed. In 2000, the average CEO was paid *531 times* more than the average worker.

Often, the biggest salaries paid to CEOs had little to do with the performance of the companies they led. In 2000, for example, Charles Wang of Computer Associates was paid $698 million, despite weak shareholder return over the previous 3 years. Walt Disney CEO Michael Eisner pulled in $699 million that year despite anemic shareholder gains.

The epidemic of excessive CEO compensation even reached beyond public companies into the New York Stock Exchange. The exchange, located at the corner of Wall Street and Broad Street in lower Manhattan, is the place where the biggest U.S. companies list and sell their stock to investors. As a marketplace, the NYSE is a not-for-profit organization run by its members, who own "seats" on the floor, enabling them to trade stocks on behalf of other parties.

During the 1990s, with the growth of the Internet, many high-tech companies decided to sell their stocks through brokers over an electronic network known as Nasdaq. But the established companies stayed on the NYSE, where floor specialists brokered practically every transaction and promised even small investors that they would get the best price available for a given stock.

The chief executive of the stock exchange, Richard Grasso, helped modernize the NYSE's electronic trading systems, so traders could buy and sell stock almost as quickly as they could on the Nasdaq electronic system. During the boom years, he steered the exchange to great profitability. Members were happy because their investment in the exchange--the value of the seats they owned--rose dramatically, topping out at $2 million per seat in November of 2002.

Because of his control over who sat on the NYSE's board of directors, Grasso could see to it that his friends served on the board's compensation committee. But while the NYSE insisted on absolute transparency for the companies that wanted their stock traded there, the exchange itself provided no information on how much money it paid Grasso. Even some board members didn't know.

It wasn't until the SEC demanded an accounting in 2003 that the exchange disclosed Grasso's salary. Over a four-year period, from 1999 through 2002, Grasso received $81 million in salary and bonuses, a princely sum for the head of a non-profit organization. Because he elected to defer some of that compensation, the CEO accumulated a one-time payout of $139.5 million.

SEC chairman William Donaldson was outraged and demanded an explanation from the NYSE's board. On the defensive, Grasso said he had nothing to do with his pay package; he was merely the recipient of the board's largesse. But a few weeks after disclosing his $139.5 million bonanza, the NYSE board dropped another bombshell: there was a separate payment program through which Grasso had accumulated an extra $48 million. This extra stash of cash, which several board members didn't know about, alienated some of Grasso's former allies. Grasso offered to forego the additional $48 million, but it was too late: in September of 2003 he was forced to step down as chief of the exchange.

He was replaced on an interim basis by John Reed, former CEO of Citibank, who was eased out of his job at the global bank after earning $293 million in 2000. To show that he had embraced the spirit of the times, Reed agreed to be paid just $1 to help restore credibility to the NYSE.

Postscript to Waksal's crime

The whole idea behind stock options is to reward managers for a job well done. But by the year 2000, the system had become perverted. Many executives, whose wealth was tethered directly to their companies' share price, focused exclusively on keeping that share price up. If the share price slipped, they lost money; if the share price rose, they became even richer.

Stock options had evolved into an untamed beast. Instead of rewarding managers for generating long-term growth, options forced executives to win *now*. Stock options gave birth to a maniacal focus on immediate success, which sometimes led to long-term failure. Executives at Enron and WorldCom destroyed their companies for the sake of hitting earnings targets.

And on Dec. 26, 2001, Sam Waksal lost his mind and tried to bail out of ImClone stock because the FDA was going to turn down the company's application to market Erbitux as a cancer-fighting drug. Waksal nearly destroyed his own company, bringing disgrace upon ImClone's top management and raising doubts about the efficacy of its drug.

At his sentencing in June of 2003, Waksal pleaded with U.S. District Judge William Pauley III: "Please know how much I have tried to do for cancer patients," he said. "These proceedings have been about commitments I did not keep. They haven't been about commitments I did keep." Waksal begged the judge to substitute community service for some of his jail sentence, but Pauley refused, giving him the full 87 months.

In February of 2004, while Waksal was serving his jail sentence, the FDA gave its approval to Erbitux. The news fueled a rise in ImClone stock price. By summer, shares in ImClone surged past $87 per share. If only Waksal had hung on to his stock, he would be a free and wealthy man today.

Chapter Two

Enron

Around Enron, he was known as the Pillsbury Doughboy, both because of his plump physique and his quiet demeanor. Unlike his boss, Jeff Skilling, or his colleague, Andy Fastow, Rick Causey wasn't given to emotional outbursts or flights of temper. Causey, the chief accounting officer at Enron, would speak deliberately, with the caution that he had learned as an accountant at Arthur Andersen earlier in his career.

It was that voice of cautious deliberation that came through on the speakerphone at Merrill Lynch on Dec. 30, 1999, when Causey was connected to a group of bankers waiting for his assurances. The bankers were fretting about an unusual deal that Enron wanted to transact that had to close in the next 24 hours.

To some of the bankers, the whole pitch smelled funny, like an attempt by a fly-by-night salesman to sell property in Florida. But Merrill wasn't dealing with a fly-by-night operation; it was dealing with Enron, one of the world's biggest energy companies, which had paid Merrill Lynch $40 million in fees that year alone. And now, on the phone to support the legitimacy of this suspicious financial manuever, was the understated Causey.

Causey didn't defend or even explain the deal that Enron's finance people had cooked up. He simply said he was aware of it and told the bankers that Enron planned to recognize between $50 million and $60 million in earnings on the transaction. He also said that Enron's auditor, Arthur Andersen, had given its approval to the deal. Causey volunteered one other nugget of information: by helping Enron achieve its earnings targets, the deal would ensure that Enron's top executives got their bonuses for the year. The bankers understood that part of the transaction loud and clear.

After hearing from Causey, the Merrill Lynch executives wrestled over whether they should proceed with the deal. Enron had proposed trading a series of electricity-related options back and forth with the bank that would result in neither a profit nor loss to either party. But the transaction was structured in such a way that Enron would be able to claim more than $50 million in earnings on paper if it went through. The reward for Merrill if it agreed to go along with this phony deal: a fee of $17 million in cash.

One Merrill Lynch banker wondered why the firm should help Enron inflate its earnings. A colleague replied that Merrill Lynch had "17 million reasons" for doing so. That logic won the day, and Merrill closed the transaction with Enron on Dec. 31, 1999. Merrill Lynch made millions of dollars in fees on the deal, Enron bragged to the public that it had once again hit its earnings targets and Rick Causey and other senior Enron executives got their fat bonuses. Everybody won, except for the investors who bought Enron stock based on the company's purportedly strong earnings.

Edifice of mirrors

Talk to any securities expert, and you'll hear the same thing: stripped of the business-specific details and the colorful personalities of the con men who perpetrate them, all earnings manipulation schemes are the same. They depend on the misrepresentation of a company's underlying financial strength. Enron was no exception, save for the complexity involved in the earnings manipulation schemes. Some companies fool investors by exaggerating their sales. Others hide their expenses, making themselves appear more profitable than they are.

But as a financial fraud, Enron was of a higher order. Its executives took a natural gas transmission company and constructed an edifice of mirrors on top of it. To outsiders, Enron appeared to be an amazing earnings machine, a showcase example of how bold, innovative thinkers could transform a humble energy pipeline company into a futuristic marketplace where any commodity--energy, paper, fiber optic capacity--could be traded.

But with the exception of its energy trading operation, Enron's apparent success was an illusion, a fabrication born of accounting trickery. The people who should have spotted this fraud early on--the auditors, the outside lawyers, the analysts, the company's bankers and even Enron's own board of directors--all fell down on the job, or watched silently from the sidelines, collecting profits by ignoring the scam.

How bad was the fraud at Enron? For the year 2000, the company reported profits of $979 million on revenues of $101 billion. But of Enron's $979 million in reported profits, less than $100 million of that sum came from legitimate business transactions where a customer paid Enron for a product or service. Close to 90% of Enron's reported profits resulted from bogus financial machinations--bank loans that had been disguised to look like sales revenues, and tax credits that exploited loopholes.

From gas pipelines to the "gas bank"

Enron's transformation from an old-fashioned oil and gas company to the biggest Ponzi scheme ever perpetrated in America seemed unlikely back in 1984, when Ken Lay became chief executive of Houston Natural Gas. After Lay acquired several other energy firms, he renamed the operation Enron. The new company was weighed down with debt and on the brink of bankruptcy. Lay, a former energy analyst at the Pentagon, tried to figure out a way to move the company beyond the low-margin business of transporting gas from one place to another. Lay felt trapped by the unpredictable dynamics of the natural gas business. If you stocked up on gas while the price was high, you'd be hurt by a drop in price. Likewise, if you ran lean while the price was low, a price spike could hurt you by forcing you to buy at the top of the market.

In 1989, with the aid of Jeff Skilling, a consultant from McKinsey & Co., Enron figured out a way to protect itself from volatility in gas prices. It formed something new, a "gas bank," which allowed Enron to buy and sell gas contracts to companies that wanted to lock in fixed prices in a volatile market. It was a brilliant innovation that enabled Enron to stay out of the trap that ensnared it a few years earlier, when it held huge inventories of natural gas at a time when prices were falling.

Like the average householder, companies with significant energy needs were at the mercy of price volatility in energy costs. Enron's gas bank allowed companies to plan ahead with Enron to guarantee a fixed amount of gas--one or two or three years down the road--at a set price. For companies trying to plan their budget needs, the gas bank removed the uncertainty from future energy costs. For producers of natural gas, who were exposed to the risk that low energy prices would hurt their earnings, the gas bank brought stability. By entering into contracts with Enron to deliver gas immediately or in the future, a gas producer could lock in a guaranteed revenue flow.

Shortly after its launch, it became apparent that the gas bank worked. Skilling, who jumped from McKinsey to Enron in 1990, learned an important lesson: Enron could reap significant rewards by moving rapidly into risky new areas and staking a claim.

Enron's business

By the mid 1990s, Enron's core business had become its energy trading operation, the same business that Skilling had created a decade earlier. It made money. But Skilling knew that Enron could not grow its stock price if it was perceived only as an energy trading operation. Prices fluctuated in the energy commodities market, and big profits one month could be followed by losses the next. For that reason, Wall Street devalued the stocks of trading companies, which had unpredictable earnings, and favored the stocks of companies that could consistently deliver 10-15% growth every year.

So Skilling diversified Enron. The company set up Enron International, acquiring and building power plants around the globe. The goal was to become the dominant energy supplier for countries that were modernizing their power grids.

At Skilling's direction, the company created a retail energy management operation, Enron Energy Services, which entered into multi-year service contracts with big clients, from sports stadiums to school districts. EES pledged to handle all of a client's energy needs, eliminating wasteful overuse of heat and air conditioning, and cutting the best deals for fuel and electricity.

And, in an attempt to turn Enron into a "dot-com" stock, Skilling launched a division called Enron Broadband, which would trade fiber optic bandwidth in the same way Enron bought and sold energy contracts. Skilling estimated that the new broadband division would add $37 to the company's share price.

The new businesses, which soaked up billions of dollars of Enron's capital, were brilliant ideas except in one regard: they lost money. That was a problem, because Enron sold itself to Wall Street as a high-growth company, always on the cutting edge. Investors flocked to Enron because of that consistent growth. Any admission that the growth was an illusion would cause investors to flee.

But Enron popped like an overinflated balloon in 2001 precisely *because* it was an overinflated balloon. At the end of 1999, the stock price approached $50 per share. The following year it would peak above $90 per share. The lofty price bore no relation to the company's weak businesses.

But Enron's top managers could not admit the failure of the new businesses to the public. They *had* to deliver earnings, not just because Wall Street demanded it, but because the bonus of every top executive depended on it. The culture of Enron, more than the culture of any other company in the late 1990s, was driven by money. Not money for shareholders, but money for top executives. In an attempt to improve performance, Enron rewarded its managers for hitting earnings targets with massive bonuses. When it recruited executives, Enron placed no priority on integrity, only on an ability to "fit in" and win. As a result, managers were focused on achieving their earnings targets *no matter what.*

By 2001, the company was salted with executives who were willing to use every arcane bookkeeping technique imaginable to claim they were hitting their profit numbers. A tacit understanding seeped throughout Enron's offices that it wasn't wise to probe too deeply into how the company hit its earnings targets. The company's top managers were aware that Skilling's new ideas--Enron Energy Services and Enron Broadband--were money-losers. But they also knew that somehow, the magicians at Enron Global Finance would rescue the company every quarter through a series of accounting transactions that defied gravity. And when Enron hit its numbers, everyone--including Rick Causey--was happy.

Tim Belden, an Enron energy trader in California, pled guilty in 2002 to fraud stemming from price gouging during the California energy crisis. Why would Belden want to rip off customers in California? Consider that in 2001, Belden's base salary was $214,000, but because he hit his performance targets, his bonus was $5.2 million.

In 2003, Wesley Colwell settled SEC charges that he manipulated earnings statements at Enron North America to disguise losses in Enron Energy Services. Colwell's salary in 2001 was $289,000, but he received a bonus payment of $1.2 million.

Colwell's boss, David Delainey, pled guilty to criminal charges associated with the same activity. His 2001 salary was $365,000, but his bonus was $3 million.

Jeff Skilling, who was promoted to CEO of Enron in 2001, earned $1.1 million in salary that year, but received $5.6 million in bonus payments. For executives at Skilling's level, stock options were also a powerful incentive to keep Enron's stock price high. Skilling cashed out $19.2 million in stock options in 2001; Enron chairman Kenneth Lay cashed out $34 million in stock options that year. The man who benefited most from his exercise of Enron stock options was Lou Pai, who cashed out $270 million in the years leading up to the company's collapse.

The $80,000 lemonade stand

Andy Fastow headed up Enron Global Finance. An ambitious executive who joined the company at age 28, Fastow impressed Skilling with his creativity in structuring financial deals. Fastow also surrounded himself with aggressive young acolytes who shared his view that accounting rules were challenges to be overcome through ingenious financial maneuvers.

To understand better how Fastow and Enron Global Finance perverted the meaning of accounting rules, imagine that your eight-year-old daughter sets up a lemonade stand in front of your house on the hottest day of the summer. As it happens, two of your neighbors are out mowing their lawns in the sweltering heat. Within five minutes of the time when your daughter sets up the stand, both neighbors come over and plop down $1 each for a big glass of ice cold lemonade. How much is that lemonade stand worth? Not much, even if other neighbors are willing to come by and overpay for their drinks.

But accountants at Enron Global Finance would note that your daughter earned $2 within the first five minutes of operations. They would assume that she'd take in $24 for every full hour of operation. By keeping the lemonade stand open for 10 hours, she'd ring up $240 for a full day. And if she kept the stand open for 365 days, she'd record $87,600 in sales revenues per year. But the lemonade mix itself would cost some money, and there might be a few days of snow or rain during which sales might suffer. So Enron Global Finance would deduct a few thousand dollars and estimate that the lemonade stand was worth $80,000 per year. And the auditors at Arthur Andersen would sign off on that valuation, because it met the letter, if not the spirit, of the accounting rules.

As ridiculous as it sounds, that's how Enron computed the value of many of its assets and contracts. In 1996, for example, Enron purchased a majority stake in a drilling company called Mariner Energy for $185 million. Over the next several years, when Enron needed to goose up its income statement, it arbitrarily assigned a higher value to Mariner. Late in 2000, for example, Enron needed an additional $100 million in earnings to meet its quarterly estimates. So several top Enron executives told their subordinates to increase the Mariner valuation by $100 million, bringing the company's value on Enron's books to $365 million. After Enron's collapse in late 2001, an internal review determined that Enron had overstated Mariner's value by at least $257 million.

Fastow's secret partnerships

Fastow's group used accounting tricks to inflate the company's income, disguise the amount of debt on its balance sheet, and pump up Enron's cash flow. It achieved all this by forming a series of private partnerships, known as "special-purpose entities," and engaging in business transactions with those partnerships.

The model for these partnerships was a joint venture formed in 1993 with Calpers, the California pension fund giant. Dubbed the Joint Energy Development Investment partnership, JEDI was a "win-win" situation for Enron. The company reduced its risk in its energy investments by finding a co-investor. Accounting rules allowed Enron to add JEDI's gains to its earnings statements. At the same time, all the debt incurred by the joint venture would, by the same accounting rules, appear on JEDI's balance sheet, not Enron's.

Enron wanted to look like a lean, efficient company to its banks. By foisting large chunks of debt into special purpose entities such as JEDI, Enron was able to make its balance sheet appear strong. It's a legitimate financing strategy, employed by airlines when they lease planes instead of purchasing them. The balance sheet of an airline that bought its own fleet of Boeing 747s would be cluttered with debt.

But finding partners to enter into ventures such as JEDI wasn't easy. When Calpers told Enron it wanted to sell its interest in JEDI in 1997, Enron had difficulty finding another party willing to put up money in a joint venture.

Energy investments are risky by nature. They're expensive, since they involve large, cumbersome assets like power plants, and their profitability depends on factors outside of the investors' control, like the market prices of oil, gas and electricity. But Fastow, who would become Enron's chief financial officer, devised a way for Enron to have it both ways. As a teen growing up in New Jersey, he was a fan of the *Star Wars* movies, which explained his decision to label the Calpers partnership "JEDI." In 1997, he formed a new investment partnership, Chewco, named after "Chewbacca," the furry sidekick to the maverick *Star Wars* pilot Han Solo.

Because Fastow couldn't find an outside investor willing to put up $383 million necessary to buy out Calpers' interest in JEDI, he formed his own investment group to raise the money. But there was a problem: as an officer of Enron, Fastow's role as an investor doing business with the company would violate standard conflict-of-interest rules.

So Fastow designated a trusted deputy, Michael Kopper, to be the nominal head of Chewco. Since Kopper wasn't an officer of Enron, there would be no need to disclose his role in the company's annual report. The only problem was that for Chewco to qualify as an independent venture--one that was exposed to the risks and benefits of its investments--outside investors had to hold a stake of at least 3% of the venture. Kopper didn't have 3% of $383 million, or $11.5 million.

So Fastow figured out a way around that, too. Kopper and his domestic partner, William Dodson, put up their personal savings of $125,000, and Barclay's bank fronted the rest. But here again, there was a problem: Barclay's considered part of its money a loan, not an investment, so even though Fastow was able to get Chewco up and running by the end of 1997 (just in time for Enron to make its numbers and reward its executives with bonuses), the joint venture wasn't legitimate.

Think of Chewco as an elaborate version of the lemonade stand. Enron claimed the stand was worth $80,000, but couldn't find any independent businessmen who agreed with that assessment, so it borrowed money from a bank and pretended that an Enron employee was an "outside investor" who believed that the stand was worth $80,000.

Enron's control of Chewco undermined the notion of "fair market value." Kopper did Fastow's bidding at Chewco, buying and selling Enron assets whenever he was told to. By appearing to be an independent third party, Chewco gave credibility to Enron's claim that its assets were worth the inflated value assigned to them. After all, if an independent businessman agrees to pay $80,000 for a lemonade stand, maybe he knows something you and I don't.

Over its first two years, Chewco allowed Enron to claim $161 million in earnings, and hide more than $600 million in debt from its investors. For Kopper, Chewco was a windfall. When the company bought him out in 2001, his $125,000 investment had swelled into $10 million. A nifty gain for someone whose only job was to serve as a front man.

Fastow still wanted to run his own private equity fund to trade with Enron, so he set up a new partnership, LJM. Fastow put up $1 million of his own money, raised another $15 million from two banks, and entered into a hedging arrangement which allowed Enron to book a $95 million paper gain from its stake in a dot-com stock. (Note: Enron didn't *earn* $95 million in cash, it simply *claimed* it on paper.)

Enron's code of conduct rules required permission from the board of directors before a senior officer could enter into a business relationship with the company. The board approved the plan, with the understanding that the company's managers would monitor Fastow's actions closely. (Management did nothing of the kind, allowing Fastow free reign to engineer all kinds of deals that benefited him personally.)

LJM--the initials of Fastow's wife Lea and his sons, Jeffrey and Matthew--was such a hit within Enron that in 1999, Fastow asked if he could form a second, larger partnership, LJM2, to enter into more deals with the company. Once again, the board approved, and Fastow raised $394 million from a series of banks and individuals. Over a two-year period, Enron did more than 20 deals with Fastow's LJM partnerhips. While the deals as well as the accounting tricks varied, the theme of all the LJM transactions was the same: the partnerships would agree to "purchase" weak Enron assets at whatever price Enron wanted. Enron guaranteed that Fastow would recoup his personal investment, no matter what. With that kind of a guarantee, LJM gobbled up as many $80,000 lemonade stands as Enron cared to sell it.

Because he was on both sides of the Enron-LJM transaction, Fastow collected enormous fees for his transactions. His 2001 base salary (before bonuses and stock grants) was $440,698, but Fastow pocketed an additional $30 million from managing the partnerships over two years.

Bank prostitution

Fastow could not have fabricated the illusion of real earnings at Enron without the support of various banks, most notably J.P. Morgan Chase and Citibank. From 1992 to 2001, Enron entered into a series of pre-pay arrangements with Chase and an offshore subsidiary, Mahonia. The deals were designed to look like commodity trades with a third party. But Mahonia was nothing more than a shell company operated by Chase, and the "trades" that Enron entered into with Mahonia amounted to a pledge that Enron would pay back, with interest, the money it borrowed from Chase. A federal judge ruled that Enron's Mahonia transactions were the equivalent of bank loans. Over a nine-year period, Chase provided $3.5 billion to Enron this way, not a penny of which showed up as debt on the company's balance sheets.

Investigators discovered an email from a top Chase banker, in which he described the game played by the bank: "We are making disguised loans, usually buried in commodities or equities derivatives (and I'm sure in other areas). With a few exceptions, they are understood to be disguised loans and approved as such."

Citibank loaned even more money to Enron, $4.8 billion. But while Chase was at risk for the entire sum of money lent to Enron, Citibank repackaged about half of its Enron loans as bonds and sold the bonds to institutional investors. Like Chase, Citibank let Enron fool investors into thinking that its balance sheet was relatively free of debt. But Citibank went a step further and sold some of that debt to outside investors who had no idea that Enron was deceiving the investing public. As one Citibank executive bragged in an email: "Enron gets money that gives them cash flow but does not show up on (its) books as big D Debt."

What's the harm in making a bank loan look like a sale of goods or services? Plenty: investors want to know what a company's true liabilities are. A company that can hide its debts appears healthier than it really is. The effect was doubled at Enron because those loans were reported on earnings statements as "sales." By disguising its loans from Chase and Citibank as energy sales, Enron fooled its investors in much the same way.

The same transactions that allowed Enron to classify the Chase and Citibank bank loans as commodity trades also had an impact on the company's cash flow statements. Over a nine-year period, Enron recorded $8.3 billion as cash from *operat-ing* activities, when the cash actually came from financing activities. The distinction is important to investors, who would much rather see a company generate cash through sales of its product than by borrowing money that has to be repaid with interest.

When Enron's problems were revealed and the company declared bankruptcy in December of 2001, Chase and Citibank were among its biggest creditors. Some of Enron's other creditors blame the two banks in part for Enron's collapse, since they helped the company disguise billions of dollars in loans.

That's the most shocking aspect of the scam perpetrated by Enron on its investors. Time and again, the company entered into transactions with respected financial institutions that should have revealed the weak state of the company's business operations. But those institutions, including Merrill Lynch, J.P. Morgan Chase and Citibank, refused to see the truth about Enron. Instead, like the Merrill Lynch banker who had "17 million reasons" to push ahead with the phony 1999 transaction, the bank executives were more concerned about the fees they generated from Enron than the company's fraudulent posture in the marketplace.

Bogus businesses

Andy Fastow engineered much of the fraud at Enron through transactions with partnerships he controlled. But he wasn't the only culprit. Executives who ran two of Jeff Skilling's pet projects--Enron Energy Services and Enron Broadband--also stretched the truth to meet earnings projections or impress investors.

The business strategy behind Enron Energy Services was to sign long-term contracts with big corporations and institutions, promising to manage all the energy needs of those entities. With its expertise in energy, Enron promised clients it could generate significant savings for them. Companies that specialize in customer service might have been able to pull it off, but Enron was not that type of organization. Enron executives excelled at talking big ideas and signing contracts, but were weak when it came to follow-through at the customer-service level.

Because they needed to show the appearance of growth, Enron signed dozens of contracts with universities, big companies and even a professional baseball team, the San Francisco Giants. For 1999, Enron claimed the total value of its EES multi-year contracts was $8.5 billion. But that figure was from the world of $80,000 lemonade stands. The money wasn't real. Enron induced most of these clients into contracts by promising huge savings it could never deliver, or paying cash upfront to the client. Customers such as JC Penny complained as soon as they saw how inept Enron was at delivering on its promises.

But Enron's claim that EES had billions of dollars worth of deals under contract impressed investors. To demonstrate the division's success to Wall Street analysts, Jeff Skilling opened the doors to the operation's "war room" on the sixth floor of the company's 50-story headquarters. When Skilling marched the analysts through, in January of 1998, the room was humming with activity. Hard-charging Enron employees worked the phones, typed orders into their computers and appeared to be negotiating with clients. But the whole thing was a show.

According to a report in *The Wall Street Journal*, Skilling modeled the analyst walk-through on the climactic scene from the movie, *The Sting*. Enron spent half a million dollars outfitting the "war room" to look like the hub of a thriving enterprise. Staffers painted phones black and computers flashed up statistics and charts of what seemed like live deals. Secretaries were recruited from other floors and told to play along. Skilling even had a rehearsal the day before to make sure everything ran smoothly.

Similarly, Enron Broadband was the product of smoke and mirrors. At an analyst conference in January of 2000, Skilling promised that it would be able to deliver high-quality video across the Internet. Ken Rice, who headed up EES and moved to broadband, said the company had the technology in place to deliver content to consumers across the country. It was a lie, as Rice subsequently admitted in a plea deal with prosecutors.

Nevertheless, Skilling told analysts that the new division would generate $1 billion in operating profits by 2004. A few months later, Enron signed an exclusive agreement with the Blockbuster video chain announcing a service that would enable Blockbuster customers to order movies with the click of a computer mouse. Enron Broadband would stream those movies into the customers' home computers on demand.

Like many of the EES contracts that promised the company billions but generated no real revenue, the Blockbuster announcement was little more than just that, an announcement. Blockbuster had nothing to lose: Enron was promising that it could deliver digital versions of movies to homes across the country. Blockbuster didn't have to put up any cash. But by December of 2000, Blockbuster realized that Enron's broadband technology was not as advanced as the company had promised. It wanted out of the arrangement.

Desperate to record sales for a business that was bleeding, Ken Rice had his accountants work with Fastow's people to create artificial revenues. Using some lemonade-stand assumptions, Enron Broadband entered into a series of deals with Fastow's partnerships that produced $53 million in phantom revenues from the venture in the 4th quarter. The following quarter, when Blockbuster finally pulled out of the deal, Enron used similar tactics to book another $58 million in revenue, for a six-month total of $111 million.

Clipped hedges

Ultimately, according to the board of directors' investigation, Enron's hedging activities--which essentially guaranteed the value of the company's risky investments--brought the energy giant to its knees. The reason was simple: Enron insured the value of its poor investments using its own stock.

There was enormous internal pressure at Enron to buy and sell assets, because that's how Fastow engineered the appearance of growth. By 2001, Enron had purchased lots of power plants that were sinking in value. The company unloaded these plants and other weak assets on Fastow's partnerships.

But the declining value of these assets threatened the partnerships themselves. So Fastow created a whole new set of partnerships, which he named "raptors," to guarantee the value of the assets. The Raptor partnerships provided the equivalent of an insurance policy to Enron that said no matter how low the value of the power plants sinks, the partnerships would guarantee the plants' full value. The only problem was that the Raptors had no capital to back up their promises. Instead, Enron capitalized the Raptors with its own stock.

What's wrong with this picture? Enron's bankrolling of the Raptors is the equivalent of writing an insurance policy on your house and using that very house as collateral for the insurance policy. You tell people that your $250,000 home is insured with a policy backed by a $250,000 piece of real estate. But you don't tell them that that real estate is the home you're insuring. So what happens if your house burns down? Your insurance policy is worthless.

As long as Enron's stock kept rising, the company's circular "self insurance" program seemed to work. But in 2001, Enron's stock started slipping--the equivalent of the house catching fire. As the value of its investments also slipped, the company approached a danger zone. Enron would have to dip into its stock to cover the losses on its investments, but its falling stock price meant Enron would have to pony up even more shares of its stock to cover future losses. The stock losses couldn't be hidden on the company's financial statements, and once the company disclosed these new losses to investors, Enron's stock price would plummet further. Enron would then have to issue even more stock to pay off its investment losses, precipitating a nasty cycle that would blow a huge hole in its earnings.

Sherron Watkins' letter

In August of 2001, with the company's stock price still sliding, CEO Jeff Skilling shocked his colleagues and investors by announcing his retirement, only six months after attaining the title he'd worked towards for more than a decade. Within days of his resignation, an executive in Fastow's finance group, Sherron Watkins, wrote an anonymous letter to Enron chairman Ken Lay. In her letter, Watkins laid bare the phony accounting that propped up Enron's earnings and warned Lay that Enron might "implode in a wave of accounting scandals."

Watkins was eventually identified as the memo's author. In a personal interview with Lay later that month, she insisted that Fastow, the Andersen auditors and Enron's law firm, Vinson & Elkins, could not be trusted to clean up the problems they'd helped create, and advised Lay to seek outside counsel to root out Enron's accounting problems. Instead, Lay thanked her and asked his lawyers at Vinson & Elkins to conduct a limited review of Watkins' concerns. Lay warned the lawyers not to delve into any of the accounting issues that so alarmed Watkins. Not surprisingly, the lawyers said that aside from some "bad cosmetics," they uncovered no improprieties.

But while the lawyers were busying themselves over "bad cosmetics," Enron's accounting problems finally came home to roost. At Andersen's insistence, Enron consolidated the Raptor partnerships on its balance sheet and announced a loss of $544 million for the third quarter of 2001. Two other write-downs involved another $500 million in losses. The surprise announcement of the red ink, just two months after the sudden resignation of Skilling as Enron's CEO, shocked even Enron's biggest boosters on Wall Street.

Despite the setback, most analysts--some of whom admitted that they never understood the company's convoluted annual reports--maintained a "buy" rating on the stock, even as its price slid from $80 down to $26. But the media, which also never understood how Enron made its money, jumped on the news. *The Wall Street Journal* disclosed that most of Enron's recent losses stemmed from secretive deals between the company and partnerships controlled by Fastow. On Oct. 23, Ken Lay staunchly defended Fastow, proclaiming he had the utmost confidence in his top finance executive. But that confidence lasted only one day, when Fastow was placed on administrative leave.

Enron's implosion

For Enron, the end came quickly. By early November, wary Andersen auditors learned that the funding for Chewco was actually a bank loan, negating Chewco's status as a special purpose entity and forcing Enron to consolidate all of Chewco's debt and losses on its balance sheet. On Nov. 8, Enron announced that it would have to restate its earnings going back to 1997, the year Chewco was formed. That announcement, coming after three weeks of unremitting criticism over revelations about Fastow's partnerships, destroyed investor confidence.

As the stock price plunged into single digits, credit rating agencies lowered the grades of Enron's debt. Banks that had been deceived about the true nature of Enron's debt obligations now called in their loans, but Enron didn't have the cash to pay off those loans. Enron chairman Ken Lay arranged a last-minute deal to sell the company to Dynegy, a cross-town rival. After reaching an agreement in principle to buy Enron, Dynegy gave the company a $1.5 billion cash infusion. But the money disappeared so quickly into Enron's trading activities that Dynegy pulled out of the merger. As November came to a close, so did Enron's options. On Dec. 2, the company filed for Chapter 11 bankruptcy protection from its creditors.

Sherron Watkins remembers the next day clearly. She and thousands of other loyal Enron employees showed up for work on Monday, Dec. 3. Enron's top managers pulled aside 5,000 staffers, and told them, in groups of 50 to 100 at a time, that because of the bankruptcy, they would have to be let go, with a payment of $4,000, just three weeks before Christmas. What the senior Enron executives didn't tell those staffers was that they--the managers--had decided to divvy up $55 million in retention bonus money among themselves. These top Enron executives, while they were tossing salaried staffers out into the street, awarded themselves sums of money that were several times their annual salaries. And to collect that money, they only had to stay with the company for three months.

"In my mind, they are just as crooked as Andy Fastow," says Watkins. "The fact that they could think about themselves and let 5,000 employees go with zippo was alarming. I didn't recognize how corrupt the culture had become."

Criminal investigations

In January of 2002, the Justice Department formed the Enron Task Force, an elite group of prosecutors, FBI agents, SEC lawyers and IRS agents, and charged it with getting to the bottom of the wrongdoing at Enron. Over the next three years, the task force charged more than 30 defendants with crimes associated with the accounting fraud. Prosecutors indicted Ken Lay,

Jeff Skilling, Andy Fastow, Ken Rice and Rick Causey, the chief accounting officer who persuaded Merrill Lynch to participate in at least one bogus transaction.

Fastow and Rice eventually agreed to cooperate with the investigation, pleading guilty to reduced charges and capping their jail terms at 10 years apiece. Two of Fastow's assistants, Kopper and Ben Glisan, also pleaded guilty, as did Fastow's wife Lea, who had been an assistant treasurer at Enron.

Ken Lay held a press conference after his indictment in July of 2004, proclaiming his innocence and vowing to fight for his good name. But the criminal charges took a toll on Skilling. After his indictment, on a visit to New York City, he and his wife spent the night drinking with people they met at their hotel bar. When the group moved to a "cigar bar" on the city's Upper East Side, Skilling became intoxicated and turned on his new-found friends, accusing them of being undercover FBI agents.

As the group dispersed for the evening, Skilling tried to rip the license plate from the car of the people he thought were federal agents. He also grabbed at the blouse of the woman who owned the car, in the hope of finding a recording device he was convinced she was carrying. When the police responded to a call concerning the incident, they observed Skilling wandering in the middle of a Manhattan street, gazing up into the night sky and talking to an imagined satellite camera he believed to be tracking his every move.

Aiding and abetting

So how could Enron convince so many people that its lemonade stands were worth $80,000 each? In the case of the Wall

Street brokerage houses that recommended Enron stock to the public, Enron used its banking fees as both stick and carrot. Until 1998, Merrill Lynch employed John Olson as its chief analyst for Houston energy companies. Olson's job was to monitor Enron's operations and determine whether the stock was worth recommending to the investing public. Unlike other analysts, Olson was skeptical of many of the company's claims. Enron executives grew annoyed with Olson in 1997 because he had dropped the stock from an "accumulate" rating to a "neutral" rating.

After Enron managers complained to Olson's bosses at Merrill Lynch headquarters, the skeptical analyst was pushed out and replaced with a new analyst, who took a more bullish view of the company. In response, Enron began throwing investment banking work at Merrill, helping it earn more than $40 million in fees that year. In return, Merrill Lynch's investment bankers, like their counterparts at Chase and Citibank, were willing to enter into deals with Enron that allowed the company to deceive investors.

Following Enron's collapse, investigators discovered evidence that bankers at Chase and Citibank were fully aware that Enron was trying to disguise loans as sales revenue. Prosecutors eventually brought charges against four Merrill Lynch bankers for participating in a bogus transaction involving electricity barges off the coast of Nigeria. In November of 2004, a jury in Houston returned guilty verdicts against the four. All three financial institutions cooperated with investigators and pledged never again to engage in the type of behavior that helped prop up Enron for so long.

But as far as Sherron Watkins is concerned, the banks' promises of good behavior are worth as much as Enron's promises of annual growth. Jail sentences for executives such as Glisan and Fastow send a powerful message to anyone thinking of cooking a company's books, Watkins says. "Part of the problem is that, with the exception of some Merrill Lynch executives, the bankers have gotten away with not being charged," she says. "Enron's schemes could not have happened without the bankers. They closed these questionable deals, and held their noses. I really want to compare these guys to Saddam Hussein claiming he was not responsible for gassing the Kurds."

And what about the auditors? In the case of Arthur Andersen, Enron paid the firm a total of $52 million per year, or $1 million per week. Enron's accountants worked closely with Andersen to make sure that the company stayed within the letter of the rules, even when it violated the spirit of those rules. Until Enron's collapse, auditing firms could claim that they too were victims in cases of accounting fraud. But as Andersen's partners would soon learn, the game was about to change.

Chapter Three

The Auditors

On the 9th floor of the federal courthouse in Houston, in the hallway outside of U.S. District Judge Melinda Harmon's courtroom, a buzz filled the air as word passed quickly that a jury of 12 men and women had reached a verdict in the obstruction of justice trial of Arthur Andersen. It was a beautiful Saturday morning, June 15, 2002, the day before Father's Day; it was about to become the darkest day in the history of the accounting profession in the United States.

The jury had been deliberating for 10 days, an excruciating wait for the prosecutors who had effectively run the firm out of business over the shredding of Enron documents the previous year. And it was an excruciating wait for Andersen's top partners, who were fighting for the one thing that had driven them throughout their careers, pride.

If there was one thing that unified Andersen's 28,000 employees across the U.S., it was pride; pride in working for the preeminent accounting firm; pride in working for an outfit that was always a pioneer, never a follower; pride in being right. But on this otherwise glorious Saturday morning in June, Andersen's pride was about to become its shame.

The jury filed into the wood-paneled courtroom. Judge Harmon asked if they had reached a verdict. Jury foreman Oscar Criner III said they had: guilty. C. E. Andrews, the Andersen partner put in charge of the firm following the resignation of CEO Joseph Berardino in March of 2002, slumped in his chair at the defense table as the judge read the verdict. Although he had nothing to do with the Enron debacle or any of the other high-profile cases where Andersen botched its job as an auditor, it was Andrews' unfortunate role to be the last leader that the 89-year-old accounting firm would ever have as an auditor of publicly traded companies. A hush came over the courtroom as the magnitude of the verdict sank in. But a thousand miles to the north, somewhere outside of Chicago, Arthur Andersen himself must have been turning in his grave.

The bad old days

Before the stock market crash of 1929, buying a stock was like buying a used car. There were no nationwide rules regarding what a company had to tell prospective investors. Then and now, investors seek companies that can succeed in the marketplace. But without reliable information about a company's prospects, investors run the risk of buying a lemon.

Congress felt that one of the reasons for the 1929 crash was the proliferation of companies that boasted strong earnings but had none at all. Stock fraud was rampant in the 1920s, as bad as anything that occurred in the Internet bubble of the late 1990s. Fly-by-night companies made outlandish claims and suckered investors into buying their shares.

In the wake of that crash, and because of the Depression that followed, Congress passed two landmark laws regarding the sale of stocks, or "securities" as they're known in the profession. The Securities Act of 1933 spelled out, for the first time, a list of conditions a company had to meet in order to be able to sell shares of its stock to the public. Among those conditions: the company had to file accurate quarterly statements about its revenues (sales) and earnings (profits on those sales). In order to assure the accuracy of those financial statements, companies had to hire an auditor to check their numbers at least once a year, for the annual report.

The other landmark law, the Securities and Exchange Act of 1934, established a set of rules regarding how stocks could be sold to the public. This act affects the sales practices of the New York Stock Exchange, as well as other regional exchanges. The 1934 act also created a government-funded regulator to enforce the new laws, called the Securites and Exchange Commission (SEC).

The laws were a great boon to the accounting industry. Up until 1933, companies hired auditors on a voluntary basis, to add a "Good Housekeeping Seal of Approval"-style endorsement to their financial reports. But after the new laws were passed, auditors suddenly had a government mandate forcing public companies to hire them.

The true believers

In every profession, be it law, medicine or religion, there is a schism between the true believers and the pragmatists. Hundreds of thousands of doctors studied medicine to heal their ailing fellows, but a lot of doctors got their diplomas because the money was good. The world of auditors is no different. There is a giant divide between auditors who developed a near religious devotion to the accuracy of earnings statements, and those who became certified public accountants because they wanted lucrative careers as partners at big accounting firms.

In the history of modern accounting, no one embodied the ideal of a scrupulously honest auditor better than Arthur Andersen, a hard-driving Chicagoan who founded his own firm in 1913. In a story that is famous within the profession, the head of one of Andersen's largest clients, a railway company, visited the young man at his office and threatened to fire him as auditor unless he signed off on some fudged numbers. Staring down the president of the railway company, Andersen declared, "There's not enough money in the city of Chicago to induce me to change that report."

The head of the railway company fired Andersen, but within months, the company was in bankruptcy. The incident crystallized Andersen's reputation for honesty, and Andersen's accounting practice flourished because of its founder's integrity, not despite it. Andersen imbued his partners with the self-confidence and backbone that he brought to the profession. The firm's unofficial motto, which Andersen learned from his mother, said it all: "Think straight, talk straight."

The passage of new laws calling for publicly traded companies to hire auditors to check their financial statements fueled the growth of auditing firms like Andersen's. The mandatory audit was designed to guarantee the credibility of earnings statements. Moreover, the securities laws of 1933 and 1934 validated Andersen's belief in the sanctity of accurate numbers.

From profession to business

After World War II, the United States emerged not only as a military colossus, but a business colossus. In the 1950s and 1960s, as the nation's biggest companies expanded, the major accounting firms expanded along with them, either by opening up offices where their clients operated, or acquiring smaller firms across the country. Until this time, auditors had occasionally supplemented their income by offering a smattering of consulting services to their clients. As the clients grew in size and sophistication, the opportunity for significant growth in consulting revenues grew as well.

In the 1950s, Andersen became a leader among auditors offering consulting services to clients. The auditing firm (now run by Leonard Spacek, who took over after the death of Arthur Andersen) embraced a new tool--the computer--to help clients run their businesses more efficiently. Specifically, Andersen worked with General Electric to help GE install a computerized payroll system in its Louisville, Kentucky offices. As U.S. companies grew and relied more on computers to help them manage their businesses, Andersen leaped into the fray to help them. The growth in computer-related consulting services, which eventually became known as information technology consulting--or IT services--marked a turning point in the history of auditing.

Up until Andersen blazed a trail with IT services, auditors were in business primarily to check the earnings statements of their clients. That's how they made their money. But the auditors' familiarity with their clients' businesses created opporunities to generate consulting fees. Auditing firms like Andersen that offered significant other services to their clients had an advantage over competing auditors.

If a company used a local auditing firm for its earnings reports, but called in Andersen to help it structure its computerized payroll systems, the Andersen team could show the client why it made sense for Andersen to handle *all* of the client's needs-- including the audit. Faced with this competitive threat from Andersen, other firms followed the leader and began offering their own consulting services. Eventually, most ambitious auditors thought of themselves no longer as green-eyeshade accountants, but as business advisors who could help their clients grow.

In the 1950s and 1960s, the growth of the consulting end of the business helped auditing firms prosper. The bull market of the 1960s sparked the birth of numerous small companies selling shares to the public, each of which would need audited books. The sudden explosion of business, without a corresponding growth in the number of competent auditors, led to the loosening of some accounting standards. In the recession that started in 1969 and ushered in the weak economic decade of the 1970s, marginal companies went bust, and aggrieved shareholders, led by plaintiffs lawyers, sued auditing firms as well as the management of the failed companies.

The most significant development of the 1970s, in terms of the auditing profession, grew out of a series of government mandates that the profession "de-regulate," at least when it came to competing for business. Starting in 1973, the American Institute of Certified Public Accountants (AICPA) eased its longstanding policy forbidding auditing firms from competing against each other for business. By 1978, all such restrictions were off.

Until then, auditing was a gentlemanly profession. Auditors didn't poach clients from each other: it was unseemly. But by the 1980s, with anti-competitive restrictions removed, auditors courted each other's clients aggressively. It was in this environment that auditing was transformed from a profession into a business. Accounting firms began using their consulting practices as profit centers, and treated the auditing function as a loss leader to help them establish the initial client relationship. If two firms were competing for a company's audit, both would submit low-ball bids in order to win the account, knowing that whatever money they lost on the audit could be made up many times over with lucrative consulting projects.

The practice of "audit shopping" was inevitable. Companies that were willing to play fast and loose with their financial statements sought out like-minded auditing firms which, for a price, would sign off on the books. This shift wasn't widespread, but it was perceptible, says Lynn Turner, who spent most of his career as a partner at a big accounting firm and served as chief accountant at the SEC from 1998 to 2001. "It's fair to say it was prevalent in first half of 1980s, and the rate at which it was increasing was sufficiently alarming to Congress that they held hearings," says Turner. As a result of Congressional hearings held by Rep. John Dingell (D-Mich.), the SEC adopted a rule forcing public companies that changed auditors to disclose whether or not they had consulted with an outside auditor for special advice. The new rule helped rein in the overt practice of audit shopping.

Come the 1990s, auditing firms booked almost half of their revenue from non-auditing consulting services. The conflict between the *auditor's* role to serve as a watchdog, and the *consultant's* role to help a company grow by any means necessary emerged as a huge issue in the profession. By the year 2000, the transformation was complete: "true believers" in the virtue of the pristine audit were outnumbered by pragmatists bent on growing their own businesses. The bold decision that Arthur Andersen had made so long before--to risk losing a client rather than sign off on distorted numbers--had become a quaint and even naïve fairy tale in the accounting profession.

Loosening the legal shackles

By the 1980s, the field of public accounting had consolidated into 8 large firms ("The Big 8"), which handled the majority of Fortune 500 companies. Cases of accounting fraud proliferated. A fraud case against Continental Vending led to a momentous decision in 1968: a federal judge in New York ruled that simply because the company's auditors had followed Generally Accepted Accounting Principles (GAAP), they weren't exempt from liability in cases of fraud.

The Continental decision led to steady growth in the number of shareholder lawsuits filed against auditing firms in the decades that followed. It wasn't until the 1990s that the tide turned. In a case between two Denver banks, Central Bank and First Interstate, the U.S. Supreme Court decided in 1994 that outside professionals, including auditors and lawyers, could not be held liable for "aiding and abetting" securities fraud simply because they advised the client. The decision meant that when investors were defrauded by a company that cooked its books, those investors could only collect damages from the parties that did the cooking. After the Central Bank case, auditors could defend themselves in court by arguing that they too, like the defrauded investors, had been deceived.

Accounting firms scored an even bigger victory in 1995. It was just after Georgia Congressman Newt Gingrich orchestrated a sweeping election victory that put control of the House of Representatives and Senate into Republican hands. The new majority, citing numerous cases where plaintiffs lawyers were harassing business owners with frivolous lawsuits, passed the Private Securities Litigation Reform Act (PSLRA). The law made it more difficult for investors to sue the management of companies where fraud had occurred. It was a momentous victory for the accounting industry, which had been dragged into a growing number of shareholder lawsuits over the previous 20 years.

For those auditors who were careless in their work, the PSLRA was a green light indicating that they would not be held liable for sloppy work. "There might as well have been a sign on the highway that said, 'One cop every thousand miles,'" says Turner, the former SEC chief accountant. "The chance of getting caught was so remote that everyone drove down that highway like it was the German autobahn."

Turner's assessment was supported by the growing number of blown audits across corporate America. The situation grew so bad that SEC chairman Arthur Levitt spoke out against what he saw as an ever-increasing manipulation of financial statements. In 1998, Levitt gave a speech at New York University warning that a culture of cutting corners in financial statements threatened the credibility of the U.S. stock markets. "Too many corporate managers, auditors and analysts are participating in a game of nods and winks," Levitt said. "I fear that we are witnessing an erosion in the quality of earnings, and therefore, the quality of financial reporting. Managing may be giving way to manipulation; integrity may be losing out to illusion."

Levitt made another important point: companies that lie on their earnings statements put added pressure on honest companies to mimic those results. "Many in corporate America are just as frustrated and concerned about this trend as we, at the SEC, are," he said. "They know how difficult it is to hold the line on good practices when their competitors operate in the gray area between legitimacy and outright fraud. A gray area where the accounting is being perverted; where managers are cutting corners; and where earnings reports reflect the desires of management rather than the underlying financial performance of the company."

Like the prophetess Cassandra, Levitt spoke the truth; and like Cassandra, he was ignored. After all, stock prices kept going up and up from 1998 to 2000. People who invested in stocks were making money, even in dot-com companies that had no profits. Why should anyone pay attention to an old grouch who just didn't "get it"? Congress certainly didn't. Just the opposite: year after year, from 1993 to 2000, lawmakers let Levitt know there would be no substantial increase in funding for his agency. Instead, while the financial markets boomed, the SEC's budget crept up an average of 6% each year, growing from $253 million in 1993 to $382 million in 2000. The total number of staffers grew only from 2,940 to 3,235 over the same period.

Levitt's speech angered members of the accounting industry, who felt unfairly maligned. But while the speech was prescient, it did nothing to stem the tide of accounting disasters that were about to rob American investors of more than $500 billion.

Auditors serving two masters

In 1997, the SEC received an anonymous letter from a whistle-blower who had recently been fired by the auditing firm PricewaterhouseCoopers. The letter writer alleged that, contrary to SEC rules, several partners at the firm's Tampa, Fla., office owned stock in the companies they audited.

For auditors, who are supposed to double-check and attest to the accuracy of their clients' financial statements, stock ownership in a client is a clear conflict of interest. If there's something wrong with a client's numbers, an audit partner who holds shares of the client's stock will have an incentive to bury the truth in order to keep the company's share price up. The SEC looked into the situation at PwC's Tampa office and found that the allegations were true. The agency then ordered PwC to conduct a nationwide investigation to determine how widespread the problem was. The results shocked the commission: PwC admitted that there were almost 8,000 similar stock ownership violations in its offices across the U.S., involving half the firm's partners. Even PwC's CEO, James Schiro, owned stock in one of the company's audit clients.

After the investigation, PwC promised to put stringent rules in place to prevent the problem from ever occurring again. But other auditing firms were less compliant. Ernst & Young had entered into a joint venture with one of its clients, PeopleSoft, that drew the SEC's attention. E&Y created a special tax software program that PeopleSoft sold to its own customers. Ernst & Young made tens of millions of dollars by servicing those contracts once the software had been sold. In return, E&Y paid PeopleSoft--its audit client--royalties on the sales.

The conflict seems obvious: if E&Y spotted something wrong in PeopleSoft's financial statements, would it risk its lucrative software marketing venture by taking a strong stand? The SEC didn't think so, and in 2002, it filed a complaint against the firm. Ernst & Young's partners, including a former chief accountant of the SEC, fought the suit, but in April of 2004, a judge handed the SEC a clear victory. The judge, Brenda Murray, blasted E&Y for conduct she deemed "reckless," "highly unreasonable" and "negligent." Further, she said that the auditing firm showed "an utter disdain for the commission's rules and regulations on auditor independence." Murray singled out three Ernst & Young partners for criticism, describing their testimony before her as "argumentative, sarcastic and not forthcoming."

Those conflicts weren't the only practices that disturbed Levitt and the SEC. Even more worrisome was the growing number of accounting "restatements" issued by publicly traded companies. When a company "restates" its earnings over a period, it's admitting that its previous statements were false. Stock prices plunge when a company issues a restatement, because investors learn they've been fooled. In the 1990s, restatements cost investors billions of dollars.

Levitt was convinced that the big accounting firms (which had consolidated from the Big 8 to the Big 5) were so focused on growing their bottom lines that their audits were becoming unreliable. As a result, in the summer of 2000, more than a year before the meltdown at Enron, he proposed a new SEC rule to force accounting firms to choose between providing consulting services to a client or auditing services. But several big firms, whose campaign contributions to lawmakers on Capitol Hill gave them enormous clout, fought the proposal aggressively.

In his memoir, *Take on the Street,* Levitt recalls a meeting he had with the heads of three of the firms opposing the rule. The top Andersen partner, Bob Grafton, spoke bluntly: "Arthur, if you go ahead with this, it will be war." But Levitt forged ahead anyway, and the battle did turn into a war. The accounting firms and their trade association, the AICPA, not only fought the rule proposal on its merits at SEC hearings, but they got 52 Senators and Representatives to write or call Levitt, objecting to the change.

Levitt went to extraordinary lengths to show Congress the dangers that lay ahead. He invited several lawmakers, including Sen. Phil Gramm of Texas and Sen. Evan Bayh of Indiana, to a private session at SEC headquarters. There, SEC attorneys showed them evidence suggesting that accountants had caved in to the demands of lucrative clients, leading to restatements that cost investors more than $1 billion.

But Levitt's warnings fell on deaf ears. So he took the battle to the states. Over several months, he held a series of hearings around the country designed to show investors that auditors who earned lucrative consulting fees couldn't be trusted to act as watchdogs. "We brought it to the public's attention that this was a venal profession," says Levitt.

It was only in November of 2000, when he learned that Congress was threatening to cut the SEC's budget if the new rule went into effect, that Levitt relented. He accepted a compromise which allowed auditors to continue to sell consulting services to their clients. But Levitt succeeded in one area of reform: the final SEC rule forced public companies to disclose in their annual reports how much money they paid their auditors for auditing services, and how much they paid for non-auditing consulting services.

The results became apparent during 2001, when the rule took effect. A group of 500 of the biggest public companies paid their auditors $3.7 billion for consulting services in the year 2000, but only $1.2 billion for auditing services. Investors in Sprint learned from the company's annual report that its auditor, Ernst & Young, was paid $2.5 million to audit Sprint's financial statements, but a whopping $64 million for consulting services. With those numbers in the public domain, investors were able to judge for themselves if an auditing firm generated so much revenue from a client that its judgment was compromised.

Consultants versus auditors

The success of Andersen's consulting business contributed to its destruction. Like its audit practice decades earlier, Andersen's consulting business emerged as the industry's leader. In 1984, consulting accounted for 28% of Andersen's revenues. In 1989, consultants--who were outnumbered by a 3-1 margin by auditors--generated 43% of the firm's business. The consultants chafed at reporting to the auditors, and the auditors began to panic.

The two groups reached an agreement which would temporarily keep them from splitting apart. The consultants formed their own group and could pursue new business independent of the auditing division. Meanwhile, the auditors would start up their own consulting business, focusing on clients too small for Andersen Consulting. There was one other provision: the two camps agreed that whichever side performed better would transfer up to 15% of its annual profits to the sibling company. At the time, the auditing division was bigger. But in the 1990s, Andersen Consulting blew by Andersen's auditors, and began making hundreds of millions of dollars in transfer payments.

The consultants eventually rebelled against this arrangement, and in 1997, they sought a divorce from Andersen's auditors. A long legal wrangle ensued, with the auditors demanding a lump sum of $14.6 billion from Andersen Consulting, and the consultants wanting to just walk away. From 1997 to 2000, Andersen's auditors fought a war on two fronts. In the courtroom, they tried to extract a heavy divorce settlement, and in the business world, the auditors suddenly found themselves at the back of the pack. For most of the 1980s and 1990s, it was the largest of the Big 8 firms. By the late 1990s, after several of the Big 8 firms merged, and after Andersen Consulting had declared its intention of leaving, Andersen's auditing practice suddenly became the smallest of the remaining Big 5.

Not used to being also-rans, the auditors worked vigorously to rebuild their business. Partners who were accustomed to providing a service in which they were experts (auditing and tax advice), suddenly found themselves thrust into an uncomfortable role: salesmen for Andersen's new consulting services. Many of the partners had already committed more than $100,000 of their own money to the firm. Their financial future was inextricably wound up with the Andersen's ability to crawl out of the No. 5 position and back to the top spot in the industry.

Late in 2000, an international arbiter handed down his decision in the messy divorce case between Andersen's auditors and consultants. The arbiter ruled in favor of the consultants,

allowing them to leave the relationship without paying anything close to the $14.6 billion settlement sought by the audi-
tors. It was a shocking setback to Andersen's top managers,
who had assured the auditors a massive windfall from the consultants.

Only one aspect of the arbiter's ruling seemed damaging to the
consultants: they would have to change their name. They could
no longer be Andersen Consulting. As subsequent events
would show, forcing Andersen Consulting to change its name
(it is now known as Accenture) was a blessing in disguise. For
investors in a series of Fortune 500 companies audited by
Andersen, there would be no such blessings in disguise.
Andersen may have dropped to last in size among the Big 5
accounting firms, but by 2001, the year Enron imploded, it held
the dubious distinction of being the unquestioned leader in the
category of "blown" audits.

The management of Waste Management's earnings

One of Andersen's most notorious blown audits involved Waste
Management, a garbage collection company, which admitted
to falsifying its earnings from 1992 to 1996. When the company
acknowledged the accounting fraud in a 1998 restatement of
earnings, investors lost more than $1 billion. As is customary
following any sizeable restatement, the SEC investigated.
Andersen turned over a massive trove of accounting documents to the commission.

In reviewing all this Andersen paperwork, the SEC made a
discovery: Andersen's auditors had, in fact, identified Waste
Management's attempts to pump up its earnings early on and
objected. But the firm allowed Waste Management executives,

including a former Andersen partner who had jumped over to the client, to talk its auditors out of their position.

SEC regulators were so outraged by Andersen's complicity in Waste Management's blown audit that they charged the firm as a whole with fraud. But Andersen learned the wrong lesson from the Waste Management affair. One of its top partners, Robert Kutsenda, was sanctioned for his role in the case and banned from auditing for several years. So Andersen found a new job for him, asking him to develop a firm-wide policy for document retention.

It was an astonishing decision, and one that would doom the 89-year-old firm. Andersen's partners decided that Kutsenda, an old fox who had been implicated in an embarassing restatement, would be put in charge of designing a new henhouse!

Andersen's complicity in the Waste Management blow-up was discovered only because old and incriminating documents were still in the files that were turned over to the SEC. But instead of implementing a new firm-wide program to encourage auditors to stand their ground against difficult clients, Andersen did something different: it asked one of its top partners to figure out a way to prevent the firm from ever getting caught by its own paperwork again. It was as if a highway patrolman had stopped a driver for speeding and warned him not to break the speed limit again. The driver, in this case Andersen, responded not by changing its driving habits but by investing in a radar detector.

Andersen paid its $7 million fine in June of 2001 and promised not to break the rules anymore. A few months later, auditors in its Houston office would be confronted with the most massive fraud ever uncovered in the U.S.

The black hole at Enron

The relationship between Enron and Arthur Andersen is the quintessential example of how the accounting industry transformed itself from being a profession that served the investing public into a service business dedicated to profits. During the 1990s, Enron grew its revenues and earnings not from its old-fashioned gas pipeline business, but from exotic accounting tricks that allowed it to book revenues today that it wouldn't receive for years.

Every step of the way, Enron convinced its auditors at Arthur Andersen that the letter of the accounting rules was more important than the spirit of those rules. It helped that throughout the 1990s, Enron had hired many of its own internal accountants from the Houston office of Arthur Andersen. Enron's chief accounting officer, Richard Causey, had been the Andersen partner in charge of the audit before hopping over to Enron. David Duncan, a young partner hired out of Texas A&M in 1981, took over the Enron account in 1997. During his years heading up the audit, Duncan was a model Andersen partner because he generated so much non-audit business for his firm from Enron.

By 2001, Enron was paying the firm $1 million per week, making it the second largest Andersen client in the world. Approximately half of that money went to auditing services, and the other half was for consulting services. Duncan was a star, and Andersen CEO Joseph Berardino named him to the firm's executive management committee. Even while the firm rewarded Duncan for his new business prowess, some Andersen veterans had misgivings about the firm's work for Enron. Two of them, Ben Neuhausen and John Stewart, let

Duncan know they didn't like Enron's aggressive approach to financial reporting. Duncan voiced agreement, but never forced Enron to back down.

An accountant in Andersen's Houston office, Carl Bass, was particularly blunt in his assessments of Enron's accounting practices. But rather than listen to Bass' criticisms, Duncan got his colleague transferred off the Enron business. As a rule, partners at major national firms who manage important clients on a day-to-day basis rely on accounting experts like Carl Bass to render difficult judgments, particularly those that the client dislikes. It's easier for an audit partner like David Duncan to deliver bad news to a client when he can claim, truthfully, that the decision was handed down to him by the experts at headquarters. But in the case of Enron, Andersen allowed Duncan, the local partner and chief "salesman" of Andersen's consulting services, to make the final decision over what Enron would be allowed to do. The results would be disastrous--for investors, Enron employees and, most painfully, Andersen's 28,000 staffers in the U.S.

The shredding of Arthur Andersen

By October of 2001, Andersen's practice of allowing Enron executives to use whatever accounting methods they chose came back to bite the firm. The decline in Enron's stock price was about to force the company to acknowledge a huge loss for the third quarter of 2001. The unexpected loss would drive Enron's stock price downwards, magnifying other losses. After years of accommodating Enron's wishes, Andersen's top accountants in Chicago finally insisted that the company "take its medicine" and acknowledge the losses hidden in its books.

Just a few months after the painful settlement with the SEC on the Waste Management matter, Andersen's top partners knew trouble was ahead. In a series of emergency teleconferences, the firm's risk experts discussed details of Enron's problems with David Duncan and others. Nancy Temple, an in-house lawyer at Andersen headquarters in Chicago, reminded Duncan and other partners in the Houston office that they should adhere to the firm's new "document retention" policy, which had been drawn up by Kutsenda, the Andersen partner sanctioned in the Waste Management affair. To Duncan, the request sounded strange: Andersen's top partners were convening emergency meetings to discuss the latest developments at Enron, the firm's second largest client. In the midst of these discussions, here was Temple reminding him and his Houston associates to keep their offices clean.

Shortly after Enron declared its loss, which led to panicked selling by investors and an SEC investigation, Duncan followed Temple's advice. On Oct. 23, he organized a massive shredding campaign designed to eliminate truckloads of Enron paperwork that had been collecting over the years. On Nov. 8, when Andersen received a subpoena from the SEC requesting that it hand over all Enron-related paperwork, Temple sent Duncan an order to stop the shredding.

But she was too late. The shredding binge, which was revealed publicly in January after Enron's collapse into bankruptcy, sparked outrage in Congress and among the public. Andersen fired David Duncan, and CEO Joseph Berardino promised the public that Andersen would transform itself into the most scrupulous of auditing firms. But after the accounting fraud at Waste Management, the government wasn't convinced.

Michael Chertoff, an assistant attorney general in charge of Enron prosecutions, reviewed the facts of the Andersen case to determine what kind of punishment the government would seek against this repeat offender. (The SEC had sanctioned Andersen in the Waste Management affair the previous June.) On March 3, 2002, Chertoff and several prosecutors met with Andersen's Berardino, the firm's general counsel and lawyers from Davis, Polk & Wardwell. The discussion turned to Andersen's relationship with the SEC. In particular, Chertoff wanted to know how the firm could be so cavalier as to destroy a ton of Enron-related documents knowing full well that the SEC would eventually subpoena those documents.

Speaking candidly, one Andersen representative explained that the firm didn't get too exercised over SEC investigations. "It's just a cost of doing business," he said. The statement infuriated Chertoff, who decided shortly afterwards to indict the entire firm. Later that month, a grand jury in Houston handed up an indictment, charging Andersen with obstruction of justice. A few weeks later, Duncan entered into a plea agreement and began cooperating with federal prosecutors.

After the firm was indicted, even Andersen's most loyal clients had no alternative but to move their business to other auditors. Andersen's top partners tried to reach a settlement with the government, an agreement that would get the auditing firm out from under the cloud of the indictment and salvage its business, but the accountants ultimately decided that the price demanded by the Justice Department for such a settlement was worse than a jury trial.

The verdict

In May of 2002, a jury of 12 Houston-area residents began listening to testimony and evidence in the Justice Department's trial of Arthur Andersen. In order to prove that the entire firm was guilty of obstruction, prosecutors had to demonstrate that one or more of the firm's partners had "corruptly persuaded" other members of the firm to shred Enron documents so that they wouldn't fall into the hands of the SEC or other lawyers pursuing civil suits against Enron.

David Duncan testified on behalf of the government, but he wasn't much help to their case. He could only say that he tried to obstruct justice by shredding documents. Andersen's attorneys, led by a colorful Texas lawyer, Rusty Hardin, argued to jurors that Duncan had cut a deal with the government and therefore could not be trusted. Several other Andersen partners, including Nancy Temple, did not testify.

In early June, jurors began deliberating, but after a week, they appeared to deadlock. Judge Melinda Harmon asked them to stay a little longer and give it one more try, because if they couldn't reach a verdict, there would have to be another jury trial on the same matter. A few days later, on June 15, the jurors returned their guilty verdict and Andersen lost its remaining clients. It was a tragic end for an auditing firm that had succeeded through most of its 89-year history based on its reputation for integrity.

Just six weeks after Andersen was found guilty, Congress passed a new securities law, known as the Sarbanes-Oxley Act, which forbade auditors from offering a wide variety of consulting services to their clients. Two years after the accounting industry and its trade group, the AICPA, had succeeded in gutting a similar SEC proposal, a much more powerful law was now on the books. Worse for the auditing industry, the Sarbanes-Oxley Act recognized that the AICPA was incapable of disciplining its own members, so it created a new organization, the Public Company Accounting Oversight Board, to regulate the nation's auditing firms. By winning the battle against regulation in 2000, the AICPA set the stage for the accounting industry to lose the war two years later.

Levitt, who tried to reform the auditing profession by passing auditor independence rules in 2000, was saddened by the way the firms and the AICPA self-destructed. "They tarnished, with the help of their trade organization, the image of the industry that won't be undone for decades," he says.

Chapter Four

WorldCom

In April of 2000, Steven Brabbs, the Britain-based director of international finance and control for WorldCom's operations in Europe, the Middle East and Africa, noticed something strange: an accounting adjustment of $33.6 million suddenly popped up on his computer screen as part of the his unit's first quarter financial results. The number, an accounting entry, appeared out of nowhere and didn't fit in. Brabbs didn't get it.

To arrive at his January-through-March results, Brabbs compiled all the revenues and costs associated with his unit's operations. He wasn't a salesman whose job it was to boost revenues, just an old-fashioned, green eye-shade accountant. Brabbs took pride in getting the numbers right, whether or not they pleased management at WorldCom's headquarters in Clinton, Mississippi.

The first thing that struck Brabbs as wrong about the accounting adjustment was that it didn't come from him or any of his subordinates. It was entered into the internal accounting computer system from headquarters in Mississippi. Worse than that, the justification for the entry seemed wrong. It was taken out of his "line cost accruals."

Many WorldCom units carried something known as a "line cost accrual" number on their books. For WorldCom, the telecommunications company that owns MCI, line costs were the single most important factor in determining profitability each quarter. Phone companies don't own all the telephone lines over which they send their customers' calls; they have to pay, or "rent," line capacity outside of their own networks. The more WorldCom pays to rent outside phone lines, the lower its profits.

Because of the complexity of dealing with phone companies around the world, and the fact that cost-per-minute rates of renting third-party phone lines were constantly fluctuating, WorldCom wouldn't know for several months what its actual lines costs for the current 30-day period were. As of July 31 of a given year, for example, WorldCom executives might finally get an exact number for the line costs incurred during the month of May.

Generally accepted accounting principles require companies to match their revenues with their costs, so in the current example, WorldCom would have had to estimate its May costs to determine its profit or loss for the period. Since those estimates were often wrong, internal accountants like Brabbs established an "accrual," or reserve fund, on their books to make up for the difference later.

The reserve account functioned like a safety deposit box, stuffed with cash, which could be used to make up for any shortfalls that developed between the time when May's costs were estimated on May 31 and when the actual costs for that month were determined on July 31. The reserve accounts are a prudent way to make sure that an unexpected spike in line costs doesn't cause profitability to plummet.

But what bothered Brabbs about the $33.6 million adjustment to his first quarter numbers was that the money came directly out of this reserve account and was reported as profit. If WorldCom had received some assurance that costs would no longer fluctuate from month to month, Brabbs could justify reducing the reserve account by several million dollars and adding that figure to his bottom line. But there was no such guarantee that prices would hold steady. He felt that his operation was now exposed to any jump in cost-per-minute phone rates in Europe and beyond.

But even the risk of that cost exposure didn't bother Brabbs as much as one last fact: the $33.6 million adjustment magically brought his first quarter profit margins into line with what WorldCom headquarters wanted to see. To any trained accountant, adjustments like that raise suspicions, because they suggest management is playing with numbers to arrive at pre-set goals, rather than accurately reporting the results of operations.

When Brabbs asked people at headquarters about the adjustment, he was told that it was made upon the instructions of Buford "Buddy" Yates, WorldCom's director of general accounting. When he contacted Yates and Yates' boss, WorldCom controller David Myers, Brabbs was told that the entry was dictated by the company's chief financial officer Scott Sullivan.

Yates and Myers leaned on Brabbs to incorporate the $33.6 million adjustment into the financial statements that had to be filed in the U.K. Brabbs refused. Like a good accountant, Brabbs would never record an entry in his company's financial ledger simply on someone's say-so. Every accounting entry had to be supported by ample documentation. A controller doesn't list his company's sales as $100 million unless the paperwork--sales receipts, customer printouts, cash received--all support that number. In this case, Brabbs would have had to see evidence that cost-per-minute rates WorldCom would be paying in Europe were holding steady. He received no documentation supporting that theory.

In May of 2000, WorldCom CEO Bernie Ebbers and chief financial officer Scott Sullivan visited England to review the year-to-date financial results for Europe, the Middle East and Africa. Using a slide presentation, Brabbs included a footnote for his results identifying the $33.6 million adjustment that had been booked in the U.S. According to a report prepared for WorldCom's board of directors, Ebbers asked what that adjustment was for. Sullivan told him it resulted from a review of WorldCom's line cost accruals. Ebbers said nothing.

As the year wore on, Brabbs dug in his heels over the $33.6 million. He alerted WorldCom's auditor, Arthur Andersen, to the discrepancy and pestered his superiors in Mississippi over it. "As you know, we are unable to substantiate this entry, and from an audit perspective need to clarify how we will treat this in the statutory financial statements at year end," he wrote. Brabbs wanted to receive documentation to support the adjustment, or he wanted the entry reversed. "I am keen to ensure we are doing this with full visibility of all concerned," he concluded.

That's the last thing that Brabbs' superiors wanted. WorldCom's top financial executives in Mississippi did everything they could to avoid "full visibility" because the accounting games they were playing were wrong. Back in Mississippi, Yates wrote to Myers, the controller, about Brabbs' nagging inquiries: "Have him deal with this in the U.K... I can't see how we can cover our own ass, much less his big limey behind."

Motels and Ma Bell

To understand why top executives at WorldCom were cooking their books by 2000, it helps to understand how the company got started. In 1983, the world of telecommunications was about to shatter. A federal judge had ordered the breakup of AT&T's monopoly on local and long distance telephone service. Starting in 1984, there would be seven regional bell operating companies ("baby" bells like New England Telephone, Bell Atlantic and Pacific Bell), each of which would have to allow long-distance carriers access to its lines.

AT&T would remain the dominant long distance carrier for years to come, but its monopoly on the business was over, and soon, aggressive competitors like MCI and Sprint would win customers by underpricing Ma Bell.

Months before the Jan. 1, 1984 breakup of Ma Bell's monopoly, a motel operator in Mississippi got together with a few partners and started a company called Long Distance Discount Services. LDDS was a telecommunications middleman: it would buy transmission capacity on telephone lines and resell that capacity to businesses and individuals.

That motel operator, who had no prior experience in the telephone business, was Bernie Ebbers, a six-foot-four-inch Canadian who'd gone to college in Mississippi and settled there after graduating with a degree in physical education in 1967. In 1985, after two years as a director of LDDS, Ebbers was named CEO.

Ebbers' lack of experience in the telecommunications industry didn't matter. As an operator of roadside motels, he understood a more important concept: bigger was better. The more motels he owned in one area, the cheaper it was for him to run those motels. Telecommunications, at least in those days, was no different.

The faster LDDS could grow, the cheaper it could sell its telephone line capacity to customers, thereby pushing sales growth to ever higher levels. Starting in 1985, LDDS began acquiring other telecommunications companies, expanding its reach beyond Mississippi. Under Ebbers' leadership, the company--renamed WorldCom in 1995 to reflect its global reach--would acquire 60 companies in just over 15 years.

But acquisitions cost money, and especially in its early days, LDDS did not have much cash at its disposal. Ebbers' solution to the problem was to finance acquisitions through his company's stock.

As long as Ebbers could convince his acquisition targets that the value of LDDS stock would increase after a purchase, he could finance his deals. After LDDS merged with Advantage Companies, a publicly traded reseller, in 1989, Ebbers' company was listed on the Nasdaq exchange. Now he could tap into the public markets for his acquisitions, as long as he could show investors that his purchases would spur the company's growth ever higher.

In the 1990s, investors grew to believe that the rise of the Internet would require companies to invest massive amounts of capital in the type of fiber-optic capacity that WorldCom offered. Investors bought into Ebbers' growth strategy.

The reason for investor bullishness on WorldCom was simple: after almost every acquisition, the company seemed to grow more profitable. No matter how big WorldCom became, its ability to swallow a competitor and generate even faster growth convinced investors that the company was a winner, and that Bernie Ebbers--the Mississippi genius who favored jeans and cowboy boots over suits and ties--could do no wrong.

The masterstroke: MCI

In October of 1997, Ebbers made the biggest gamble of his life, a bet that riveted the business world: WorldCom offered the equivalent of $40 billion in stock to buy MCI. It took almost a year to close the deal, but when the merger finally took place, Ebbers had transformed his little Mississippi company into a telecommunications giant rivaling AT&T. At the end of 1998, MCI WorldCom's annual revenues were $17.6 billion.

Once again, investors believed in Ebbers' ability to turn the whole into something greater than the sum of its parts. Through aggressive cost-cutting and greater efficiency across the board, WorldCom promised that it could improve its numbers by integrating MCI's operations seamlessly into its own.

But after the MCI acquisition, Ebbers' strategy of growth through acquisition ran into a problem: how do you keep acquiring once you've swallowed the biggest fish in the pond? Ebbers' solution was to swallow whatever fish was left. In October of 1999, he reached an agreement to acquire Sprint, AT&T's other long-distance rival. This time, investors thought Ebbers had extended himself too far. WorldCom stock dropped in response to the bid. Regulators in the U.S. and Europe opposed to the move, and in the summer of 2000, Ebbers withdrew his offer for Sprint.

Ebbers' strategy of growth through acquisition seemed brilliant, but it was predicated on one rule: WorldCom's stock price could never be allowed to deflate, otherwise the company wouldn't be able to keep up its acquisition binge. And if the time ever came when WorldCom stopped acquiring other companies, its growth would slow considerably and its stock price would suffer.

After the Sprint deal collapsed, WorldCom's shares slumped. The stock, which reached a high of $96.77 midway through 1999, dropped to $46 a year later. By the end of 2000, the stock had sunk to $18.66 per share, a stunning decline for a company that provided long-distance telephone connections for a large percentage of the U.S. market.

Master and commander of the board

The role of WorldCom's board of directors was to oversee Ebbers' management of the company. But after Ebbers' remarkable series of successful acquisitions, the board came to believe he could do no wrong. By the late 1990s, the board of directors--consisting largely of executives from companies acquired by Ebbers--had ceased being a monitor of any kind.

When WorldCom consummated its deal to acquire MCI in 1998, Ebbers' power was beyond the reach of his board. Instead of regular, quarterly scrutiny of Ebbers' performance, board meetings devolved into a series of passive, rubber-stamp sessions where Ebbers' opinion carried the day. If Ebbers said WorldCom had to acquire a certain company, the board simply went along with his wishes, without doing the due diligence required to determine whether the deal made sense.

A court-appointed bankruptcy examiner zeroed in on two examples where WorldCom's board of directors abdicated their responsibility for monitoring acquisitions:

• In 1999, WorldCom bought SkyTel communications for $2 billion. The board of directors approved the acquisition after hearing a 15-minute presentation by WorldCom's management, and without receiving any paperwork to document the strategic or financial justifications for the deal. Board members told the examiner that the lack of paperwork or time spent discussing the acquisition wasn't important, given that the deal was worth "only" $2 billion.

• In 2000, shortly after his bid for Sprint failed, Ebbers wanted to acquire Intermedia. His ostensible goal was to get hold of a company subsidiary, Digex. But he was driven to do the deal simply to keep a competitor, Global Center, from acquiring the same business.

In his haste to get the deal done, Ebbers launched an expensive, last-minute bid for the company. On Aug. 31, a team of WorldCom representatives met with counterparts from Intermedia and Digex. After spending less than 90 minutes on due diligence, the companies agreed on a $6 billion price tag. Intermedia gave WorldCom a 24-hour-window to approve the deal.

Ebbers convened a board meeting on Sept. 1 for approval. Instead of making a detailed presentation to board, explaining why it made sense for WorldCom to spend $6 billion to buy Intermedia, the directors were given a quickie, 35-minute presentation and asked to sign off on it. Three years later, one director told the bankruptcy examiner that given the short amount of time allotted, "God himself could not have made the decision in one day."

Ebbers' right-hand man, Scott Sullivan, had promised the directors that WorldCom would be able to unload the portion of Intermedia it didn't want for $3 billion. But by March of 2001, the value of Intermedia's non-Digex assets had plunged to less than $1 billion. Asked by the bank examiner's lawyers about the Intermedia deal, another director said, "Pardon me while I throw up."

Ebbers' money troubles

At the same time that WorldCom's ineffective directors were rubber-stamping the deal to buy Intermedia, they were also loaning money to Ebbers. Over a 19-month period, while WorldCom's own stock was sinking and its profitability started to vanish, the board loaned Ebbers some $400 million dollars.

In the 1990s, while he and WorldCom were flying high, Ebbers invested hundreds of millions of dollars in a series of luxury ventures. He purchased a 500,000-acre cattle ranch in British Columbia for $65 million. He acquired another 540,000 acres of timberland in Mississippi, Tennessee, Louisiana and Alabama for $600 million, bought a mine-sweeping company for $14 million and spent another $25 million to convert it into a manufacturer of luxury yachts. He even purchased a half interest in a minor league hockey team, the Jackson Bandits. Ebbers also acquired a Louisiana rice farm, a lumber mill, a marina and a building in downtown Chicago.

Ebbers made all these purchases--totaling nearly $1 billion-- with bank loans, pledging his WorldCom stock as collateral.

But just because Ebbers had transformed himself from small-time motel operator into a big-time telecommunications CEO didn't mean he understood anything about yacht-building, cattle ranching, or the economics of minor league hockey. Like a kid in a candy store, Ebbers appeared to have bought these properties because he could, not because they were good investments. As his properties bled money, Ebbers' banks demanded higher levels of cash from him.

Ebbers could have sold some of these assets at a loss, but he didn't want to accept that humiliation. Nor did he want to sell his WorldCom stock, either. As a policy, he frowned on sales of WorldCom stock by his top managers, even if the sale was necessary to cover debts. But faced with the prospect of selling his privately owned businesses or selling WorldCom stock to make the necessary payments, Ebbers looked to his board of directors for help.

In September of 2000, just after approving the shotgun marriage with Intermedia, the board of directors advanced Ebbers a loan of $50 million to relieve him of the pressure he felt to sell company stock to meet his banks' margin calls. The board also awarded him a cash bonus of $10 million.

Before the month was out, Ebbers came back again, looking for more. After being turned down by the board, Ebbers went ahead and pledged a future sale of stock, generating $70 million in proceeds. But at the time of this sale, Ebbers and other insiders knew that WorldCom was not going to make its quarterly numbers in October. Lawyers advised WorldCom not to allow Ebbers to sell his stock just before the negative earnings announcement, but the CEO went ahead anyway, without any interference from WorldCom's board.

The loans to Ebbers continued into the next year, even while WorldCom's financial condition deteriorated. Several board members told the bank examiner that Ebbers' personal financial woes eroded their confidence in him. Indeed, the fact that Ebbers was spending so much time protecting his personal investments and trying to keep the banks at bay demonstrated that during WorldCom's most challenging period, Ebbers was not devoting himself 100% to his primary job. In April 2002, with WorldCom's growth foundering and Ebbers' loans exceeding $400 million, the board of directors finally acted in the interests of shareholders and fired him.

Cutting corners

The fundamental flaw in Ebbers' strategy to grow WorldCom was its absolute dependence on mergers and acquisitions. As an operating business, the company was poorly run. Without acquisitions (Ebbers was so addicted to this type of growth that he named his own luxury yacht "Aquasitions."), investors and analysts could compare the company's revenues and profits to the prior year's performance.

Such apples-to-apples comparisons would not reflect well on WorldCom's top managers, so they fudged the company's numbers. Beginning in 1999, CFO Scott Sullivan's top lieutenants, David Myers and Buford "Buddy" Yates, started transferring "line cost accruals" from the safety deposit box to the bottom line. That's what sparked Steven Brabbs' curiosity in England in April of 2000.

Brabbs wasn't the only internal accountant who was suspicious of the fund transfers. Also in April of 2000, Yates approached David Schneberger, director of international fixed costs, and told him to make a $370 million adjustment to his books for the first quarter. Yates justified the request by saying it came directly from Sullivan, "the Lord Emperor, God Himself." But Schneberger wouldn't go along with the scheme, and even refused to give his bosses the account number they needed to make the transfer themselves.

In order to get around Schneberger's honesty, Yates turned to one of his subordinates, Betty Vinson. Vinson approached an analyst who worked in Schneberger's division and asked for the account number. She claimed that she had discussed the matter with Schneberger and that everything was okay. She got the number and on April 21, one of her subordinates, Daniel Renfro, transferred $370 million from the "line cost accrual" safety deposit boxes to bottom line profits. The accounting trickery helped WorldCom claim that it had met its earnings targets for the quarter.

Capitalization of line costs

By the end of 2000, WorldCom's accounting magicians had bled the "line cost accrual" safety deposit boxes dry; they started to look elsewhere to manufacture profits. According to court documents, in 2001 Sullivan allegedly cooked up a new scheme to bolster the company's earnings: the "capitalization" of line costs.

In the late 1990s, during the "dot-com boom," investors and managers thought that the growth of the Internet would continue indefinitely. Telecommunications companies like WorldCom benefited from this belief because they owned and operated many of the roads that constituted the "information superhighway."

In order to keep up with the Internet's growth, WorldCom spent aggressively to build out its network of telephone lines in all directions. It also entered into long-term contracts with other telecommunications companies to make sure it had access to their phone lines. But when the "dot-com boom" turned into a bust in 2000, WorldCom was stuck with all the contracts for telephone line "capacity" that it had signed.

It was as if WorldCom, in its rush to become the dominant toll-collector on the information superhighway, signed contracts to buy and build as many extensions to this highway as possible. But once the Internet bubble collapsed, traffic on these extensions to the information superhighway petered out. All that was left were the long-term contracts that WorldCom and other like-minded telecommunications companies had to pay for.

Sullivan's solution to WorldCom's problem was to capitalize these network capacity costs, rather than expense them. According to generally accepted accounting principles (GAAP), companies have to deduct their expenses from their revenues every month and every quarter. Those deductions give investors an accurate idea of how much money a company has to spend in order to achieve its revenues.

Capital expenditures are an exception to this rule. When a company makes a long-term investment in a new factory or new machinery, it doesn't have to record that investment as an expense that gets immediately deducted from revenues. It gets to "capitalize" the investment, and amortize it (by deducting 4% or 5% of the investment per year) over a long period of time.

The difference is significant. Investments that are "capital-ized" have only a small effect on quarterly profits (about 1% in many cases). But 100% of a company's expenses have to be deducted from those same quarterly statements. By shifting line cost expenses into a different accounting category--capital investments--WorldCom was able to fool investors into think-ing it was much more profitable than it really was.

In the first quarter of 2001, WorldCom capitalized $544 million of its line cost expenses, distorting its earnings upwards. In the second quarter, the company capitalized another $560 million in line cost expenses. Brian Higgins, an accountant in the capi-tal reporting division, was so disgusted with the decision that he started looking for another job, according to the board's investigation. The number grew to $743 million for the third quarter, with another transfer of $841 million occurring for the final three months of 2001.

The fraud unravels

In March of 2002, just a few months after Enron blew up, the Securities and Exchange Commission launched an inquiry into WorldCom's books. Investigators at the SEC were puzzled that WorldCom didn't seem to be suffering from the same financial devastation that was blowing holes in the earnings statements of other telecommunications companies.

Based in part on the SEC request, WorldCom's director of inter-nal audits, Cynthia Cooper, started looking closely at the com-pany's books. In May Cooper and her team discovered $2 bil-lion in accounting entries that didn't make sense: WorldCom had booked the sum as capital expenditures during 2001, but the money didn't seem to have been authorized. Puzzled,

Cooper and her auditors scoured WorldCom's computerized central accounting system to determine who had allocated the funds and what they had been spent on.

Not only did they come up empty-handed, they discovered another $500 million that had been labeled as a capital expenditure on computers. Like the $2 billion before it, there was no documentation to support the entry.

On May 29, the auditors met with Sanjeez Sethi, director of financial planning. He described the $2 billion capital expenditure as "prepaid capacity," a term that Cooper had never heard before. Sethi referred the auditors to David Myers, WorldCom's controller. Myers tried to quash the internal audit, sending Cooper emails on June 4 and June 5 suggesting that she snoop around elsewhere.

A week later, Cooper told Myers' boss, Scott Sullivan, what she was up to. Sullivan explained that "prepaid capacity" meant that the company had capitalized its line costs. According to a report prepared for the board of directors, Sullivan asked Cooper to put off her inquiry until the third quarter, "because there were some things senior management needed to 'clean up' regarding capital expenditures in a restructuring planned for the second quarter."

But Cooper didn't give up. Most alarming to her and Gene Morse, a subordinate who uncovered the unusual accounting entries in the central computer system, was the fact that the prepaid capacity accounting entries were made in large, round-dollar figures. Legitimate accounting entries, based on the real expenditure of funds, tend to be fractional and exact.

On June 17, Cooper and another subordinate, Glyn Smith, finally confronted WorldCom's top accountants about the strange entries marked "prepaid capacity." Betty Vinson, who made some of the entries herself, admitted that she didn't have any supporting documentation and recommended that they speak to her bosses, Buddy Yates and David Myers.

Yates said he wasn't familiar with the entries and pushed the two toward Myers. When Cooper and Smith arrived at Myers office, he told them he didn't have any documentation supporting the entries either. According to an internal memorandum of the meeting, Myers said the entries were determined simply by what final earnings number WorldCom needed to report for the quarter.

"David [Myers] stated there were no specific accounting pronouncements supporting these entries," the memo reported. "David also stated that they probably shouldn't have capitalized the line costs but once it was done the first time it was difficult to stop. David indicated that he has felt uncomfortable with these entries since the first time they were booked. Glyn [Smith] asked David how this would be explained to the SEC and David stated he had hoped it would not have to be explained."

Cooper took her findings to the board of directors. They were shocked to learn that $2 billion in WorldCom expenses for line capacity had been classified as capital spending. According to the board's post-mortem report on accounting fraud at WorldCom, the abuses uncovered by Cooper and her internal auditors were an extension of the same types of accounting tricks discovered by Brabbs two years earlier in England. At the time, Brabbs had no idea that the strange $33.6 million accounting entry he saw was part of a global scheme directed out of Mississippi to inflate the company's earnings.

When confronted with charges of accounting fraud by Cooper and the board of the directors in June of 2002, Sullivan defended his decisions. The man who had been anointed one of nation's top chief financial officers insisted he could justify the accounting principles behind his decisions to capitalize expenses if the board gave him a few days. Over the ensuing weekend, Sullivan composed what he described as a "white paper" defending his actions. But the board, as well as WorldCom's auditors--Arthur Andersen and KPMG--dismissed Sullivan's arguments out of hand.

The board fired Sullivan the next day, June 25, stating that WorldCom had improperly accounted for $3.8 billion in expenses as capital expenditures. It also announced that it planned to restate its financial statements for 2001 and the first quarter of 2002. In England, Brabbs followed the news closely. Suddenly that strange $33.6 million accounting entry from two years earlier made sense. He wrote to his supervisor, Lucy Woods, explaining that despite his reluctance to include the entry on his books, his U.S. superiors told him that the entry "had been made at Scott Sullivan's direct instruction."

Two months later, federal prosecutors in Manhattan indicted Sullivan on charges of securities fraud. Four of Sullivan's subordinates--Myers, Yates, Vinson and Troy Normand--pleaded guilty to participating in WorldCom's scheme to inflate earnings.

In July of 2002, after acknowledging that its earnings had been overstated by billions, WorldCom filed for Chapter 11 bankruptcy protection from its creditors, the largest such filing in U.S. history. The bankruptcy filing wiped out what had once been $100 billion in market capitalization. The board's subsequent investigation determined that between 1999 and 2002, WorldCom's internal accountants made "more than $9 billion in false or unsupported accounting entries...in order to achieve desired reported financial results."

On March 1, 2004, Sullivan pleaded guilty to fraud charges stemming from his actions at WorldCom. As part of his plea agreement, he agreed to cooperate with the government's investigation of Ebbers. The next day, Ebbers was indicted on securities fraud charges. He pled not guilty and went to trial in early 2005.

Chapter Five

Tyco

The face of Karen Mayo Kozlowski, a statuesque blonde in her early 40s, was a portrait of anguish. Her normally sparkling blue eyes were bleary from lack of sleep and her face was flushed red. She sat upright in her customary seat in a dingy, poorly ventilated courtroom on the 13th floor of the dilapidated state courthouse in lower Manhattan, scarcely able to contemplate the fate that awaited her husband that day.

It was Friday morning, April 2, 2004, and the news from the previous few days frightened her. The trial of her husband, former Tyco CEO Dennis Kozlowski, as well as Tyco chief financial officer Mark Swartz, had begun six months earlier and dragged on through the frigid New York winter.

In the middle of March, the case was finally handed over to the panel of 12 jurors who had dutifully endured hundreds of hours of tedious testimony and a blizzard of exhibits. After one week of deliberations, the jury appeared deadlocked. Karen Kozlowski had hoped for a mistrial to be declared then, but the judge urged the jury to press on. They did, and over the next few days, the jurors inched closer to guilty verdicts on several of the 32 counts of larceny and fraud that the defendants faced. Now, on this Friday morning, a verdict seemed imminent. All Karen Kozlowski could do, as she braced for the inevitable, was pray.

A difficult trial

The Manhattan District Attorney's prosecution of crimes at Tyco illustrates the difficulty of bringing cases against executives who allegedly ripped off their company's shareholders.

Tyco differs from Enron and WorldCom in significant ways. The accounting fraud at Tyco did not distort the company's earnings to the degree that occurred at Enron and WorldCom. Instead, the company's top executives--Kozlowski and Swartz-- lavished tens of millions of dollars worth of bonuses on themselves that weren't disclosed to shareholders. Only when Tyco's board of directors learned of a secret $20 million payment from Kozlowski to one of their own--for brokering a $9.2-billion acquisition--did they hire a law firm to look into the way Tyco was being managed.

In the spring of 2002, the board finally discovered how much money Kozlowski had awarded himself and fired him. A few months later, directors ousted Swartz. Based on the findings of the outside law firm--the board retained David Boies, who represented Vice President Al Gore in the 2000 Florida recount-- Tyco's directors brought a civil suit against Kozlowski and Swartz.

Boies and his law firm concluded that Kozlowski and Swartz deceived Tyco's board of directors and helped themselves to hundreds of millions to which they were not entitled.

Manhattan District Attorney Robert Morgenthau came to the same conclusion, and charged the duo with more than 30 crimes. In an indictment, Morgenthau's office claimed that the Kozlowski and Swartz had run a "criminal enterprise" and looted the company of $600 million in salaries and stock options.

In October of 2003, the case against Kozlowski and Swartz made its way to the courtroom. As the first major trial of a disgraced CEO following the collapse of Enron, the proceedings promised to provide some measure of revenge on behalf of the investing public against robber baron executives who had gorged themselves on shareholders' money.

The prosecution had built its case quickly, in a matter of months after the two executives were fired. Now, a year later, as the matter was going to trial, the D.A.'s office seemed to have an unbeatable hand: they would march a parade of witnesses into court who would testify that Kozlowski and Swartz repeatedly made financial decisions to benefit themselves and a core group of insiders.

Testimony at the trial would show that Kozlowski and Swartz used a corporate "relocation" program to house themselves in luxury apartments in New York City. From 1997 through 2000, Kozlowski rented a Manhattan apartment on Fifth Avenue for $264,000 per year, all of which was paid for by Tyco and its shareholders. Publicly, Kozlowski made it appear as though he still worked out of his company's modest New Hampshire offices. Eventually, Kozlowski bought his own luxury apartment in Manhattan.

Using Tyco funds, he paid $16.8 million for an apartment at 950 Fifth Avenue, spent $3 million on improvements, and topped it

off by paying $11 million to have the place furnished by a deco-
rator chosen by his wife. When the decorator finished her
work, the apartment boasted a $6,000 shower curtain; a $15,000
dog umbrella stand; a $6,300 sewing basket; a $17,000 traveling
toilette box; a $2,200 gilt metal wastebasket; a $2,900 set of
coathangers; and a $1,650 notebook. There was also a $445 pin-
cushion.

But during the trial, Kozlowski's lawyers presented explana-
tions for the lavish spending. They pointed out that the apartment was a corporate asset, and that the Tyco CEO simply
wanted to have it furnished in a style appropriate for luxury
dwellings on Fifth Avenue. The $6,000 shower curtain, after
all, wasn't for him. It was in the maid's room.

Kozlowski told friends that he didn't know the place was going
to be decked out so exotically. When the decorator finished her
work, Kozlowski thought the place looked like a room at the St.
Regis Hotel in Manhattan. On one of his first visits, as he
arrived at the apartment after work, he spied a large table, on
top of which sat the $17,000 toilette kit. Kozlowski told friends
that he simply grabbed the decorative piece and stuck it under
a sink, so he could leave his briefcase on the table.

Defense lawyers scored points with the jury by arguing that
the two executives hid nothing from the board of directors,
claiming that the board had approved their salaries and bonuses. Several former directors testified at the trial, claiming they
had not approved such staggering sums. But the defense
lawyers tripped them up on cross-examination, getting several
to contradict, or rethink, minor elements of their testimony.

The board's duties

Jurors in the Kozlowski trial developed different opinions as to whether the former CEO and his sidekick broke the law, but they all agreed that Tyco's board of directors did a miserable job protecting the interests of shareholders. One juror, 79-year-old Ruth Jordan, concluded early on that the board members were trying to hide their own incompetence by blaming everything on the two defendants.

The job of a board of directors is to oversee a company's management. The board hires the CEO (and fires him if necessary), sets his salary and provides its own independent review of the work done by the company's outside auditors. That's the way it's supposed to work, at least.

But the accounting scandals of recent years have exposed a significant flaw in the American system of corporate governance. The chief executive often nominates his (or her) own candidates to serve on the board of directors. Instead of providing independent oversight, those board members tend to be loyal to the CEO and passive in their supervisory duties.

At Enron and again at WorldCom, compliant boards of directors flunked their most basic tests. When Enron's Jeff Skilling asked the board for a special waiver to allow finance chief Andy Fastow to run a partnership that would do business with the company, board members approved the plan, asking only that Enron's managers (the ones who concocted the idea) provide adult supervision.

When WorldCom CEO Bernie Ebbers ran into trouble with his personal investments, resulting in a margin call that would require him to sell stock, he asked the board of directors for a $50 million loan, and the board agreed!

If Ebbers had been forced to sell $50 million worth of stock, investors would have acted on the news. They would infer that he had lost confidence in the company's future or realize that Ebbers had squandered much of his personal fortune on bad investments. Either way, they would conclude he was no longer fit to be CEO. Rather than share such information with investors, WorldCom's directors kept it hidden.

Like their counterparts at Enron and WorldCom, Tyco's directors betrayed little interest in the details of how the CEO managed the company. In the late 1990s, as the accounting tricks took root at all three organizations, the stock of the three companies posted outsized gains for investors, as well as board members. Thus, the apparent success of the companies that needed the most oversight resulted in a laxness which permitted all kinds of questionable behavior.

"The board of directors system in this country doesn't work," says Sherron Watkins, who pointed out Enron's internal problems to chairman Ken Lay, then watched helplessly as Enron management mishandled the company's implosion. "It's like having a volunteer fire department. If the town is small enough, it works. But in a city the size of Albuquerque, it doesn't work, unless all the townspeople participate."

A criminal birthday party?

Prosecutors knew that defense lawyers would challenge the basic thrust of their case, that Kozlowski and Swartz looted Tyco without the knowledge of board members. From the opening arguments in the trial onward, the defendants stubbornly hewed to that line. In particular, the defense argued, Kozlowski had cleared many of his most egregious loans and bonuses with one board member, Philip Hampton, who had since died.

The district attorney's office faced another challenge at trial: keeping 12 jurors focused on an avalanche of interoffice memos and conversations in connection with the obscure accounting rules that Kozlowski and Swartz were supposed to follow in awarding bonuses and company loans.

To inject some color into the proceedings, prosecutors splashed examples of Kozlowski's lavish lifestyle on a projection screen in court. In particular, Morgenthau's office wanted jurors to experience a Tyco-funded birthday bacchanalia that came to symbolize an era of corporate greed.

The prosecution called Barbara Jacques to the stand. Jacques, who planned corporate events at Tyco, testified that in December of 2000, Kozlowski asked her to plan his girlfriend Karen's 40th birthday party at a luxury hotel in Sardinia. Jacques also admitted that she had had an intimate relationship with Kozlowski more than a decade earlier, when he was still married to his first wife.

Kozlowski often mixed business with pleasure, hosting corporate functions in exotic places like Auckland, New Zealand, Palm Beach and Athens. Most of these bashes rewarded hard-working executives with a combination of rah-rah business dinners and outdoor recreation calculated to spur them to new heights of productivity.

Even with this impressive history of planning functions for the boss, Jacques surpassed herself on the birthday party. In June of 2001, some 75 guests descended on the Cala di Volpe hotel in Sardinia ($900 per night for a room) to begin a weeklong celebration. As the guests arrived for the evening, they were ushered towards the poolside bar for cocktails by a small battalion of men dressed up as Roman gladiators.

Jacques hired dozens of perfectly proportioned models, male and female, who were dressed in period costumes. Stern-faced men carrying spears stood sentry at various positions, clad in the armor of ancient soldiers. Other men wore nothing more than flesh-colored speedo bathing suits, which left little to the imagination. One modern-day Adonis stood on a platform and flexed his muscles slowly, a Roman version of the young Arnold Schwarzenegger who drew stares from the female guests.

While the party-goers mingled on the poolside patio, stunning women in loosely flowing togas glided by, undulating their hips and offering drinks and grapes to the revelers. The women, each of whom could have been a model from a glossy fashion magazine, wore garlands of fig leaves in their hair. The band, providing the perfect melody for the occasion, struck up an old classic: "Summertime, and the living is easy..."

But for many guests, the most memorable moment at the party came during a visit to the vodka bar. The hotel had propped up an ice sculpture of Michaelangelo's David at a table with cocktail glasses. A waiter standing behind the statue poured Stolichnaya vodka into the sculpture, and the liquor then streamed out of David's penis into a waiting glass below. The imbibers giggled as their glasses were filled. If the party was designed to recall some of the glory and excess of ancient Rome, it succeeded.

As the sun began to set, candles floating in the pool twinkled and the torches burning on the pavilion waxed bright. The guests moved into the dining area. The party's host, Dennis Kozlowski, took the microphone and welcomed everyone with the surprise announcement that he and Karen, whom he had been seeing for several years, had married just five weeks earlier. The announcement sparked a burst of applause from the guests, half of whom were personal friends of the Kozlowskis and half of whom worked at Tyco.

For this party, Kozlowski's friends and subordinates were encouraged to spend the week cavorting on the Grotto Smeralda. Kozlowski even arranged to have his racing yacht, the Endeavor, with its marble fireplace and full-time crew of nine, harbored nearby. In welcoming his guests, the Tyco CEO said, "It's going to be a fun week, sailing on the Endeavor, tennis, golf, eating, drinking. All the things we are best known for."

After dinner, Karen Kozlowski's favorite music star, Jimmy Buffett, took the stage to play. For the two-hour set, Buffett earned $250,000. When Buffett finished, the male and female "servants" performed an interpretive dance. As bright flashes of light captivated the audience, the toga-clad beauties gyrated rhythmically around the pool, returning again and again to a central point where the Adonis model, wearing angel wings, sparkled.

In the final, culminating act of the performance, gladiators carried a huge cake decorated in the image of a woman's body to the center of the pavilion. Sparklers fizzed from the breasts carved into the cake. As the entire group watched, the sparklers burnt down and the frosting breasts on the cake exploded. The party concluded with a fireworks display in Karen's honor, capped by a bowman shooting a flaming arrow into a distant partition which flashed the message, "Congratulations, Karen and Dennis."

Days before the party took place, Kozlowski arranged for a board meeting to occur during his stay on Sardinia. He and Swartz convened the meeting at the hotel, and piped in other directors via speakerphone. In court, Jacques testified that Karen Mayo Kozlowski's 40th birthday bash cost $2.1 million. Because he had invited so many Tyco employees and held a brief board meeting, Kozlowski charged half the cost to the company.

Prosecutors secured a four-hour videotape of the party, which they tried to play in court. But state judge Michael Obus sided with defense lawyers, who protested that footage of the vodka-spewing ice sculpture and other salacious images would prejudice jurors against their clients.

The judge finally allowed an edited videotape, lasting about 20 minutes, into evidence. The prosecution, which hoped to fill jurors with revulsion over Kozlowski's alleged abuse of corporate funds, miscalculated badly. Several jurors said after the trial that the events portrayed on the videotape didn't offend them at all. If anything, the Sardinian bash bored them, spurring several to question whether prosecutors had any real evidence of crimes by the defendants.

One juror, Glenn Andrews, noted that Kozlowski had entrusted a former girlfriend, Barbara Jacques, with the job of creating a blow-out party for his bride-to-be, Karen Mayo. The fact that Kozlowski could still rely on Jacques as a loyal supporter long after their affair had ended impressed Andrews more than anything else about the party.

A brilliant career

The criminal charges against Kozlowski brought an unsavory halt to what had been a phenomenal career. The son of a New Jersey transit system detective, Kozlowski grew up in the hard-scrabble city of Newark. He attended nearby Seton Hall University, where he majored in accounting, and paid his way partly by playing guitar in a local band, under the nickname "Kid Kelly."

Beginning in 1970, Kozlowski worked in a series of auditing jobs in New York and New Hampshire. In 1975, he joined Tyco Laboratories where his career took off.

During the 1980s, Kozlowski proved himself an able manager, and was eventually named Tyco's president and chief operating officer. After taking over as CEO in 1992, Kozlowski decided to ramp up the company's growth rate and calculated, correctly, that Tyco's profits and its stock price could rise much more quickly if Tyco acquired other companies, stripped out excess costs and folded them into its own operations.

To that end, Kozlowski began an acquisition binge that continued through most of his 10-year reign as CEO. In 1994, he spent more than $1 billion to buy Kendall International, a manufacturer of disposable medical supplies. It was a relatively new business for Tyco, but Kozlowski's instincts paid off: Kendall soon began contributing strongly to the company's bottom line, increasing Tyco's profits and helping the company's share price grow.

Tyco made its money by being a big player in unglamorous businesses like commercial construction, electronic equipment and medical supplies, but there was nothing unglamorous about Kozlowski's life. As a rising young executive, Kozlowski, who already had his pilot's license, learned to sail. He bought an expensive boat and moored it the exclusive Corinthian Yacht Club in Marblehead, Massachusetts. Since he traveled frequently, he also developed a taste for fine wines and gourmet dining.

His frequent travels also meant that he was spending less time with his wife and two daughters. Although he was not handsome in a movie-star sense, Kozlowski attracted women, especially those who worked for him. During his trial, Jacques and another former Tyco employee testified that they had had relationships with Kozlowski on his way up the ladder at the company.

By the mid 1990s, as Tyco's stock kept climbing higher, Kozlowski grew rich from the value of his Tyco stock options. He plunged headlong into a life of opulence. The kid from the wrong side of the tracks in Newark had become rich enough to afford anything he desired. Over a five-year period, from the end of 1996 through 2001, Kozlowski took home aproximately $286 million in cash and stock as the company's chairman and CEO.

To his friends, particularly his drinking buddies, Kozlowski was a good guy. He never pretended to be something that he wasn't, and didn't take on airs, despite his enormous wealth. On summer nights on Nantucket, he and Karen would listen to the music of Ecliff and the Swing Dogs. Kozlowski liked the band so much that Tyco often hired the group to play its events.

But Kozlowski's openness and candor with his friends belied a stealthy campaign to hide his runaway spending at Tyco from the prying eyes of shareholders, the media and some of the company's directors. In 2001, when he was living large in Manhattan, Kozlowski bragged to a *BusinessWeek* reporter that at his company's New Hampshire offices, "We don't believe in perks, not even executive parking spots." Even in the company's annual reports, Kozlowski boasted to shareholders that his focus was on growing the company and keeping costs down.

Despite the talk, Kozlowski lavished relocation loans on his top executives, even when they didn't need them. Kozlowski hired Mark Belnick, a prominent lawyer who made his name during the Iran-Contra hearings in the 1980s, to be Tyco's corporate counsel in 1998. Even though Belnick aleady owned a home in the New York suburb of Harrison, some 25 miles from the city, Kozlowski allowed him to borrow $2.6 million to purchase a luxury apartment in Manahattan. Belnick subsequently used $9.4 million more from Tyco's relocation loan program to buy a dream house for his family in Park City, Utah.

Corporate loans are much more attractive than bank loans and mortgages, because the rates are generally lower and the lender is more flexible. Default on a bank loan at your peril, but if you have a good relationship with the CEO, then maybe he'll forgive all or part of your corporate loan.

That's what happened with Barbara Jacques, Tyco's corporate event planner. Jacques received a corporate loan of $500,000 to move from Tyco's former headquarters in New Hampshire to New York. When she left the company, Tyco forgave the loan, giving her complete ownership of the expensive Manhattan apartment that the company had paid for. (After criminal charges were filed against Kozlowski, Jacques paid the company back for the loan.)

In other instances, Kozlowski seemed to engage in self-dealing. For example, Kozlowski caused Tyco to buy his New Hampshire home for $4.5 million, even though its appraised value was only $1.5 million. The company eventually ate the $3 million loss. During his trial, prosecutors presented evidence that Kozlowski even used Tyco's resources to find--and pay for--a summer apartment in Madrid for his college-age daughter, who was doing a semester abroad.

Kozlowski was generous with Tyco's funds. As CEO, he gave away $106 million to various charities. Some $43 million of these contributions resulted in his name being slapped on buildings at his alma mater, Seton Hall, and Berwick Academy, a private school in Maine that his daughters attended.

Then there's the money Kozlowski showered on Karen Mayo, whom he met while she was waiting tables at a New Hampshire restaurant. According to the Manhattan District Attorney, in 1997, three years before he divorced his first wife to marry Mayo, Kozlowski provided her with $100,000 in Tyco money, presumably so she could buy a New Hampshire condominium. Two years later, Kozlowski gave her $1 million in Tyco funds.

After taking up with Kozlowski and moving with him to Boca Raton, Mayo used Tyco money to open her own restaurant in

Florida, called Zemi. During Kozlowski's trial, prosecutors presented evidence that Kozlowski purchased $57,000 worth of gift certificates from the restaurant with Tyco funds.

Beginning of the end

After the stock market turned bearish in 2000, Kozlowski lost his magic touch at Tyco. His last great acquisition, of ADT Security Services in 1997, had allowed him to relocate Tyco's legal incorporation to Bermuda. The offshore base would eventually save the company as much as $600 million per year that it would otherwise have paid in U.S. taxes.

In 2001, Kozlowski acquired CIT, a financing company, for $9.2 billion. The acquisition was a disaster, since Tyco overpaid for a company that wasn't growing. Tyco subsequently sold it for a huge loss. But the acquisition also undermined the board's confidence in its CEO. Kozlowski had made the purchase at the recommendation of a Tyco board member, Frank Walsh, who was friendly with CIT's chief executive. As a "finder's fee," Kozlowski gave Walsh $20 million. It was a payment that outraged the other directors, and it posed a conflict of interest for Walsh.

As a director, Walsh's job was to protect the interests of shareholders. But who cared about the shareholders when there was a chance for a $20 million score? The other directors demanded the money back, but Walsh wouldn't budge. At a tense board meeting in Boca Raton, when the other directors asked for the money back, Walsh stood up, said "*adios*," and left the room, resigning his position. Kozlowski's other allies on the board now began to doubt the CEO's judgement. They hired an outside law firm to review Tyco's business practices. Walsh eventually pleaded guilty to one criminal charge for accepting the money. He subsequently paid it back and testified against Kozlowski at trial.

The seeds of the criminal charges against Kozlowski were planted in 2001, when he decided to furnish his $17 million Manhattan apartment with masterpieces of fine art. Just as Kozlowski had misjudged the value of CIT and overpaid, he was about to make buying decisions about paintings that he had no business making.

Kozlowski's love of the good life may have given him a discerning palate for fine wines, luxury yachts and other trappings of wealth. But these passions provided scant defense in the opaque world of fine arts, where it's almost impossible for a novice to determine the fair price of a given work.

According to a profile in *The New Yorker*, Kozlowski claimed that on the advice of an art consultant named Christine Berry, he bought a Monet seascape for $4 million, a Renoir for $4.7 million, and several other paintings by famous artists for a combined $4 million. But instead of paying for the masterpieces himself, Kozlowski used Tyco funds. His explanation: since the paintings were to be displayed in the company's luxury Manhattan apartment, they were company property.

Kozlowski allegedly tried to dodge the New York state sales tax on the art works. Because Tyco maintained a base of operations in New Hampshire, which has no sales tax, the game supposedly cooked up between Kozlowski and the art dealer was simple enough. The art dealer shipped boxes that appeared to contain the art to the company's New Hampshire offices, where a Tyco employee signed for them. The Manhattan District

Attorney subsequently accused the art dealer of shipping empty boxes, while the artwork itself was sent to Kozlowski's Manhattan apartment. The Monet, which was hanging at an art dealer's apartment at 930 Fifth Avenue, was simply moved up the block to Kozlowski's place at 950 Fifth Avenue.

Morgenthau's prosecutors stumbled onto this case of alleged tax evasion while pursuing an unrelated investigation into money laundering. The art transactions initially appeared suspicious because the art dealer who sold the Monet to Kozlowski wired the $4 million to an offshore account. In response to a subpoena, the dealer provided paperwork surrounding the transaction, including one receipt which said, "sales tax is not applicable (wink, wink)."

The D.A.'s office soon learned that the piece of art in question was, in fact, hanging in the New York apartment occupied by Kozlowski. Once the D.A.'s office located the painting, it issued subpoenas regarding Kozlowski's other art purchases. By the end of May, 2002, Kozlowski learned that he was going to be indicted for evasion of sales taxes.

Just before the indictment, Kozlowski delivered the commencement address to St. Anselm College in Manchester, N.H. His words to the graduating class are telling: "As you go forward in life you will be confronted with questions every day that test your morals. The questions will get tougher, and the consequences will become more severe. Think carefully, and for your sake, do the right thing, not the easy thing."

When the Tyco board learned of the indictment, it fired Kozlowski and intensified the investigation into his activities as chairman and CEO. Using an internal investigation, Tyco's board of directors claimed that Kozlowski had employed over-ly aggressive accounting tactics to make many of the company's acquisitions look better than they were.

The finale

Kozlowski opted not to testify at his trial, but his co-defendant, Mark Swartz, did take the stand. Throughout the six-month process, the lanky former finance officer was a foil to his former boss. Kozlowski, a stocky executive with a bullet-bald dome for a head, would sit impassively at the defense table, acknowledging the seriousness of the process. During breaks, he would chat quietly with his lawyers or his wife.

The effervescent Swartz, who had a full head of curly black hair, always seemed to be smiling. His parents and in-laws often joined his wife and three children in the courtroom. He even made eye contact with some of the jurors, exchanging a discreet nod with Glenn Andrews at the start of each day's proceedings.

Swartz performed masterfully on the stand, explaining under gentle questioning by his own lawyer what he had done at Tyco. Even under cross-examination, Swartz held his ground, talking around specific points the prosecutor threw at him without sounding evasive. Swartz was so impressive that during closing arguments, assistant district attorney Ann Donnelly compared him to a glib talk show host.

Swartz's testimony, and the arguments of the defense lawyers, raised serious doubts among some of the jurors. Even after six months of testimony and exhibits, the 12 had difficulty agreeing on whether or not Kozlowski and Swartz had committed any crimes. After a week of debate and discussion, one juror stopped deliberating with the others. According to other jurors, Ruth Jordan was sympathic to defense arguments through the trial, and she believed that Tyco's directors were at fault for allowing the defendants to help themselves to the $600 million.

Fearing a hung jury, New York state judge Michael Obus called the jury into his courtroom to urge them to continue to deliberate. On the way in, Jordan reached up with her right hand to brush her hair away from her forehead. It appeared to some members of the press that she was flashing an "ok" signal to the defendants' table.

Two newspapers--the *New York Post* and the *Wall Street Journal*--broke with long-established tradition and published the juror's name, identifying her as the holdout and stating that she had appeared to make the "ok" signal to the defense. Despite her new notoriety, Jordan promised the judge that should could continue to deliberate. For the next few days, she did, and the jury listened to a reading of key portions of Swartz's testimony.

By Thursday evening, April 1, the questions coming from the jury room suggested that the panel was close to convicting both defendants, at least on some of the counts. Karen Kozlowski, who had been so hopeful of a mistrial the week before, expected the worst.

But when Ruth Jordan got home that evening, she found a letter criticizing her stance in the trial. Ever since her name had been published as the "holdout" juror, the court was concerned about threats to her safety. On Friday morning, as Karen Kozlowski prayed in the courtroom, Jordan told Judge Obus that the letter disturbed her. He declared a mistrial. Jordan subsequently gave an interview to the TV program *60 Minutes II* in which she said that because of an unusual medical condition, she constantly brushed her hair back from her face. She said she was not making any kind of gesture to the defense table. But she felt in her heart that the defendants were not guilty.

The retrial of Kozlowski and Swartz began in January of 2005.

Chapter Six

HealthSouth

Bill Owens, an overweight finance executive with a double-chin, struggled to keep up with his boss. HealthSouth CEO Richard Scrushy moved from a conference room at the company's Birmingham, Ala., headquarters towards his office. It was March 18, 2003, and time was running out. The company had to file an earnings statement with the Securities and Exchange Commission within a few days and Owens was afraid.

HealthSouth executives had exaggerated the company's profits for years, making a poorly run company look like an earnings machine. Under a new federal law, the Sarbanes Oxley Act, it was a federal crime for someone to sign off on bogus earnings statements. Owens, HealthSouth's chief financial officer, didn't want to affix his name to the SEC filing.

Owens suffered from depression. At lunch that day he drove home and spoke to his wife about his dilemma: should he sign the SEC documents and break the law? Or should he come clean to the securities cops about HealthSouth's finances and hope for leniency? Owens' predecessor on the job, Weston Smith, wrestled with the same troubling questions. If Smith was cooperating with the authorities, then Owens was in deep trouble.

On this Tuesday afternoon at HealthSouth's headquarters in Birmingham, Owens wanted guidance from the company's charismatic leader. He had tried to get that guidance in the morning, but his conversations with Scrushy went nowhere. Owens and Scrushy presided over a 2:30 meeting of the company's officers, after which Owens tracked his prey.

At 4 p.m., he got a few minutes alone with his boss. He told Scrushy he was scared of what might happen if he lied to the SEC, but that if he didn't lie, if he avoided signing the documents that week, "all hell would break loose." Scrushy sounded sympathetic, but firm. "You ought to be able to engineer your way out of what you engineered your way into," he said. "Does that make sense?"

Scrushy also confided that he had trouble sleeping at night, wrestling with the threat to his company. "Look at how profitable this company is," he said, apparently arguing against disclosure. "Do we really want to trash all this?" Scrushy urged Owens "to go down fighting. You know what I mean?"

Why tell the SEC that HealthSouth's finances weren't all they were cracked up to be? Other companies played the same games, Scrushy reasoned. "I am convinced that there are 8,000 companies out there right now that have shit on their balance sheets," he said. "Everyone I've been involved with, everyone I know, everybody does."

The conversation continued for a few more minutes, then Scrushy and Owens went to another meeting. But Owens could relax now. It sounded as though Scrushy had spoken to him about HealthSouth's cooked books, and Owens had recorded everything on a device provided by the FBI. Scrushy's lawyers would eventually argue that there was an innocent explanation for everything he said to Owens that day. Shortly after 5 p.m., Owens left the office, ready to plead guilty to securities fraud, and hoping his cooperation with a federal investigation of HealthSouth would lead to a reduced sentence. That evening, after Scrushy departed, FBI agents raided the company's headquarters and seized documents from the executives' offices.

On March 19, the SEC filed civil charges against Scrushy, accusing him of masterminding a scheme to overstate HealthSouth's earnings by at least $1.4 billion. In the ensuing weeks, Scrushy was fired and more than a dozen former HealthSouth executives pleaded guilty to criminal charges stemming from the fraud. In November, 2003, the U.S. Attorney in Birmingham unsealed an 85-count criminal indictment against Scrushy, alleging that he was responsible for overstating HealthSouth's profits by $2.7 billion from 1996 through 2002.

An Alabama success story

Richard Marin Scrushy, who had risen to become one of the wealthiest and most successful CEOs in corporate America, started off as a nobody pumping gas in Selma, Ala. The teenager didn't show much promise as a businessman. He married his high school girlfriend after she became pregnant, and took various jobs, from gas station attendant to day laborer before he realized he needed to get his college degree if he was going to amount to anything.

With guidance from his mother, he decided to become a respiratory therapist. He moved to Birmingham, and attended Jefferson State Community College and the University of Alabama. When he graduated, he combined his knowledge of respiratory therapy with his god-given gifts of persuasion and began to teach. A few years later, he landed a job with Houston-based Lifemark Corp., which operated hospitals on a for-profit basis.

It was at Lifemark that Scrushy's innate business skills began to blossom. In short order, he was promoted head of his own division. It was also at Lifemark that Scrushy began to hone his talent for motivating employees.

In 1983, Congress changed the law concerning how Medicare would reimburse health care providers. Under the new rules, health care providers that specialized in specific areas of coverage, who could keep their overhead low, would be favored. Instead of paying a hospital back for all the services provided to a patient, as well as a portion of the overhead for empty hospital beds, Medicare would only pay a defined amount specifically aimed at reimbursement for services rendered. The new rules presented challenges for general service hospitals.

Scrushy saw a business opportunity where others didn't: starting a new kind of health care company that specialized in physical rehabilitation. He anticipated that a new generation of health-conscious Americans was hitting middle age, staying active by jogging, bicycling, swimming and playing other sports. As these baby boomers got hurt, they would need physical rehabilitation facilities. Scrushy suggested to top management at Lifemark that the company start a physical rehabilitation division that he would run, but the company refused. So in 1984, he enlisted a few partners and with $50,000 founded HealthSouth.

An aggressive salesman with a knack for motivating people around him, Scrushy quickly grew HealthSouth into a multi-million-dollar business, taking it public in 1986. Scrushy also had a well-tuned instinct for promotion, seeking out as rehabilitation patients high-profile athletes such as Bo Jackson and Roger Clemens. The sports superstars enhanced the company's credibility among weekend jocks.

Scrushy grew HealthSouth in much the same manner as Bernie Ebbers grew WorldCom: by acquiring other companies and slashing costs. The driving force behind the acquisition spree was Scrushy's vision of physical rehabilitation as a glorious crusade.

Prior to the founding of HealthSouth, physical rehabilitation was an afterthought in the world of medical services. In a system dominated by general service hospitals, the most important services centered around a facility's stars: surgeons and general practice doctors. Physical rehabilitation was relegated to dark and dingy interior rooms, a sign of the science's second-class status.

Scrushy built and acquired facilities where physical rehabilitation ruled: the centers were bright and modern. Service-oriented doctors and nurses made patients feel like stars. Scrushy even wrote his own book, *How I Changed the Rehab Industry*.

Many of his colleagues and top managers considered the charismatic CEO a genius. One of HealthSouth's former chief financial officers, Aaron Beam, Jr., applied for a job with

Scrushy when he was at Lifemark. The meeting left a lasting impression on him. More than a decade later, in an interview with the *Birmingham News*, Beam said, "I went home and told my wife that I just interviewed with the biggest con artist I ever met, or the most brilliant young man I ever met. Either way, I was taking the job because he was really, really good at what he did."

Beam signed on with Scrushy and eventually helped launch HealthSouth. In 2003, years after his retirement, he pleaded guilty to one count of bank fraud at the company.

Living in a dream world

Everyone has dreams, visions of themselves as movie stars, rock-and-roll singers, sports heroes or other exalted figures. Once Scrushy became rich from the early success of HealthSouth, he began to turn his own dreams into reality.

He learned to pilot his own plane, and through his focus on sports rehabilitation, rubbed elbows with sports stars like Troy Aikman and Dan Marino. Renewing a childhood interest in rock music, he started a band with other HealthSouth executives, which he playfully called Proxy. (Public companies issue annual "proxy statements" to their shareholders to keep them abreast of changes in management, and allow them to vote on a slate of directors.)

In the early 1990s, Scrushy took his dreams of media stardom to another level, forming a country band called Dallas County Line, and flying professional musicians into Birmingham from Nashville twice a week. Scrushy, the lead singer, cut his own rock video to the tune of "Honk if you like to Honky Tonk." In

1995, Scrushy played the video at HealthSouth's annual meeting, and even took his band on the Dallas County Line Down Under Tour to Australia. According to court documents, most of the money for Scrushy's foray into pop music came from HealthSouth.

After divorcing his second wife, Karon Brooks, Scrushy took up with a HealthSouth staffer named Leslie Jones. In 1997, he flew 150 guests to Jamaica for their wedding. Included on the guest list were Emmylou Harris and Martha Stewart.

Scrushy's showmanship extended to official HealthSouth business. In 1996, he launched the "Go for it!" roadshow, a traveling exhibition featuring famous athletes preaching the virtues of healthy living and moral fiber to kids. The show was initially popular with young people and grade school teachers.

But Scrushy couldn't leave well enough alone: in 2000 the success of the roadshows convinced him that he could use the events as a launching pad for a musical "girl group" modeled on Britney Spears' act. He found a music producer in Orlando, Fla., and launched "3rd Faze," a band featuring three young women warbling tunes aimed at junior high and high school girls.

Scrushy pushed the band and paid for the production of its first CD, which was launched to coincide with the debut of the company's "Go For It" TV show on the USA network on Sept. 15, 2001. According to the official history of HealthSouth, Scrushy also cut a deal with Sony music chief Tommy Mottola that would send a stream of Sony's music artists to appear on the HealthSouth program. With a foot in the world of pop music, Scrushy attended the Grammy awards, hob-nobbing with the country's biggest music moguls and stars.

Scrushy's fascination with stardom and his attempt to turn the "Go for It" exhibitions into a TV show led him to cross paths with a former childhood TV star, Jason Hervey, who played the mean older brother Wayne in the sitcom, *The Wonder Years*. Hervey and Scrushy clicked immediately, and Scrushy eventually convinced the former actor to give up his life as a Hollywood producer and move to Alabama, where he could head up HealthSouth's communications department.

In Birmingham, Scrushy and Hervey made for an odd couple. The pair were in constant communications at HealthSouth, sending Blackberry messages back and forth to each other, not about business matters, but about where they would spend their weekends together with their wives. But where Scrushy's third wife, Leslie, a preacher's daughter, was devoutly religious, Hervey's wife was a former porn star.

On weekends, they would fly out to Scrushy's compound on Lake Martin, about 70 miles from Birmingham. There, they could frolic at Scrushy's Mediterranean-style villa, or take turns zipping around the freshwater lake in one his cigarette speedboats, a practice that local boaters, with their smaller craft, despised. Or Scrushy and his entourage would venture further afield by flying to another compound on Alabama's gulf coast, or jet to Palm Beach, Florida, where Scrushy kept his 92-foot luxury yacht, Chez Soiree, moored.

Then, back at the office, Scrushy and Hervey would discuss their exploits on a weekly radio show they hosted every Tuesday night. In these shows, Hervey called Scrushy "Cowboy" and the older man referred to the former TV actor as "Gator." With his riches from HealthSouth, Scrushy had turned himself into a rock star, TV producer, radio jock and miniature music mogul.

Nowhere was this more apparent than at Scrushy's home, a baronial estate located in the suburb of Vestavia Hills, just outside of Birmingham. There, Scrushy would welcome visitors by ushering them into the "media room." On the wall of this room hung a huge painting of Scrushy cruising along a highway atop a Harley Davidson motorcycle, wearing a bandana and looking like Dennis Hopper in the movie *Easy Rider*.

Once visitors had a chance to absorb the image on the wall, Scrushy insisted they sit and watch his music video, one that he claimed had reached the No. 1 position in Australia during his "Down Under" tour. The video, featuring Scrushy singing "Honk if you like to Honky Tonk," includes cameo shots of Neil Diamond and other celebrities.

Cooking the books

According to the federal indictment, the $2.7 billion fraud at HealthSouth began at least as far back as 1996. Unlike the fraud at Enron, which resulted from insidious accounting trickery designed to fool even sophisticated investors, HealthSouth's fraud was more basic. Every quarter, the company's corporate staff determined what HealthSouth's actual earnings would be, then compared that result with the earnings Wall Street analysts expected.

Instead of missing the number and taking their medicine--a hit to the stock price--HealthSouth executives gathered together in a special meeting to fabricate different financial results. The company's executives described these meetings with code words, calling them "family" meetings, where they would identify "gaps" or "holes" in HealthSouth's earnings and fill those holes with "dirt."

According to testimony she gave to Congress, Diane Henze, vice president of finance, first noticed the unusual last-minute adjustments to earnings in 1998. When the practice continued into 1999, she objected to her boss, assistant controller Ken Livesay.

"You can't tell me that we have enough reserves to reverse that would justify this type of swing in the numbers," Henze told him. "When he told me that I was right, I informed him that I did not understand what was going on, but would have no part in any wrong-doing. Ken apparently went to Bill Owens, the controller, with my suspicions because Bill called me in an attempt to justify what they were doing. Bill said that HealthSouth had to make its numbers or innocent people would lose their jobs and the company would suffer. I told Bill that I believed that whatever was going on to be fraudulent, and I would not participate in it and wanted no part of it. I also asked him to stop whatever it was they were doing and told him that I was going to keep an eye on it."

Henze lodged a complaint with HealthSouth's compliance department, but her protest drew no reaction. Later, after she had been passed over for a promotion, she complained to Owens. "I was told by Bill that he could not put me in that position, because I would not do what they wanted me to do," Henze said.

It would happen every quarter, Henze recalled. Just before earnings were announced, a group of HealthSouth finance executives would meet in the conference room outside of Bill

Owens' office. Then, shortly after the meeting broke up, Henze would receive a phone call telling her about accounting adjustments that were to be made, which always boosted the company's earnings, never lowered them.

According to forensic accountants and other fraud investigators, earnings manipulation schemes like the one at HealthSouth can't be pulled off by one or two rogue executives. They usually involve a dozen or more people who, for a variety of reasons, sign on to the scheme. What makes these otherwise respectable executives break the law? They're not bank robbers, who slide notes to the teller demanding money. The act of robbing a bank is the brazen, desperate act of an individual who's willing to risk a long stretch in jail for a small amount of cash.

White collar criminals are another matter. They don't pop out of bed in the morning, stretch their arms and resolve that day to violate federal securities laws. Just the opposite: they're often conscientious people who want to do the right thing. They've worked hard through their careers, and achieved success.

But somewhere along the way, when their company's earnings slipped slightly for the quarter, they ventured into a gray area. Maybe they discovered an unusual accounting loophole and exploited it, squeezing extra earnings into the quarter and solving the company's problem. The boss liked that, giving them a big raise for their ingenuity.

Then, in the next quarter, the company's sales slipped again. Now the boss approaches them directly, imploring them to do whatever they can to help the company meet its earnings expectations. This is the point where ingenuity sometimes metamorphoses into criminality. If the numbers-crunchers are honest, and report that earnings are down for the quarter, they've failed, at least in the eyes of their superiors.

That's what happened to Diane Henze at HealthSouth. She missed out on a promotion because she wouldn't play the game. But the internal accounting and finance people who devised another ingenious way for the company hit its earnings targets became heroes.

In order to take that final, criminal step, most white-collar criminals tell themselves they're doing it because they're intimidated by the boss; or they're doing it "for the good of the company." Another favorite rationale is that they'll "only do it once." The next quarter, sales will rebound, and the company will report honest earnings. At least that's what they tell themselves.

The opposite usually occurs. A company like HealthSouth that's having trouble hitting its earnings targets one quarter will most likely miss those targets in subsequent quarters. But since HealthSouth appeared strong, investors bid the stock price up with the expectation that earnings would keep growing. Thus, every quarter, it became even more important for HealthSouth's finance executives to bridge the gap between the real earnings and what Wall Street expected. And as any crook can tell you, when you've broken the law once to create fictitious earnings, it doesn't take much to get you to do it again.

Armed with cooperators like Weston Smith and Bill Owens, federal prosecutors in Birmingham quickly reached plea agreements with 15 members of the HealthSouth "family" who participated in the fraud. U.S. Attorney Alice Martin listened as each of these admitted felons tried to explain why they broke the law: some didn't want to lose their jobs; others felt pressured by the boss; still others thought that HealthSouth's outside auditors had approved of the creative accounting. But faced with the prospect of jail time, each admitted his or her guilt.

In all, five men who served as chief financial officer admitted to their role in the scam, blaming Scrushy for their actions. To defend himself, Scrushy appeared on *60 Minutes* and declared that he was an innocent man, duped by underlings who were out to line their pockets. But by the time the fraud was exposed, Scrushy had lined his own pockets, selling much of his stock for $100 million. These stock sales were over and above his annual salary and the $53.6 million in total cash bonuses Scrushy received between 1996 and 2003 as a reward for leading HealthSouth to what was believed to be strong profitability.

Security and paranoia

Around Birmingham, people often referred to Scrushy as "King Richard." As the head of a Fortune 500 company and one of the top-paid CEOs in the country, Scrushy was concerned about his personal safety.

Although he owned dozens of exotic collectible cars, as well as a small fleet of Cadillac Escalades and Hummers, Scrushy drove around town in a $120,000 bullet-proof BMW. At HealthSouth's headquarters, he had Jim Goodreau, his chief of security, install hidden cameras on the 5th-floor executive level. He also used Goodreau for unusual security details, urging him in an email message to spy on the activities of a fellow HealthSouth board member, Joel Gordon.

When driving to work in the morning, Scrushy used a special access road that took him into the company's parking garage. There, he would enter the building's elevator and activate a code that allowed him to shoot directly up to the 5th floor, without stopping for passengers at other floors. Common employees needed a special pass to gain access to the 5th floor. In this way, Scrushy avoided contact with the vast majority of his workers.

When it came to criticism, Scrushy had a thin skin. A former employee named Kimberly Landry criticized HealthSouth management on an online message board in 1998, and the company sued her for defamation. A few years later, when another HealthSouth employee, Michael Vines, posted negative opinions about HealthSouth anonymously on a web site, Scrushy ordered Goodreau, his security director, to identify the source of the postings.

Scrushy's fear of betrayal wasn't completely misplaced. In late July of 2002, he learned that William Massey, his personal accountant who worked in an office at Scrushy's family compound, had embezzled $500,000 from him.

Scrushy's temper could reduce HealthSouth employees to tears when they didn't achieve the company's goals. For members of his inner circle, like Massey, it was worse. Scrushy confronted Massey late that July, wanting to know the full extent of the theft. Then he summoned Massey's mistress, Hope Launius, who also worked at the compound, demanding to know if she was in on the thievery.

With the money he had embezzled from Scrushy, Massey had been living his own fantasy life. While his wife and two children were safely squirreled away in their suburban Birmingham home, Massey swept Launius off her feet and away from her husband, showering her with expensive gifts and squiring her around the country on Scrushy's private jet.

Scrushy wanted to know if Massey's fraud went deeper than the $500,000. Massey said no, and Launius insisted she knew nothing about the embezzlement. She confessed only to bad judgment for straying from her husband and sons in pursuit of the good life.

Within days, Massey seemed to have crumbled under the pressure. When he spoke to Launius, she recalled how shaken he looked. She noticed that his mouth seemed completely dry and his lips stuck to his teeth. He was a beaten man. On the morning of July 30, according to a police report, Massey drove to a deserted corner of the suburb where he lived, stuck a shotgun in his mouth, and pulled the trigger.

Following the suicide of a once-trusted lieutenant, Scrushy pursued Launius. Not only did the loss of $500,000 anger him, but the attractive 35-year-old's relationship with Massey seemed like a personal betrayal: she was a good friend of his wife's and had helped her build her own maternal lingerie company, Upseedaisies.

But try as he might, Scrushy couldn't get Launius to admit that she was part of the embezzlement, so he took his threats a step further. He told Launius that if she ever wanted to see her two sons again, she'd better shut up about what happened with Massey. Otherwise, Scrushy would do everything he could to get custody of the two boys transferred to Launius' estranged husband.

Scrushy reduced Launius to tears by his interrogation and threats, but a few months later, she extracted her revenge. In the fall of 2002, after angry HealthSouth investors complained that Scrushy had sold nearly $100 million in stock prior to a negative news announcement crippled the company's earnings, Launius contacted lawyers at the Securities and Exchange Commission and told them that Massey had been deeply concerned about Scrushy's sales of stock.

The SEC investigation eventually turned into the criminal investigation that exposed HealthSouth's long-running fraud and resulted in Scrushy's firing and his indictment. The former CEO's trial began in Birmingham in January of 2005.

Televangelist

In March of 2004, just months after being indicted, Scrushy returned to the airwaves. Under the auspices of the Guiding Light Church, Scrushy purchased 12 months worth of airtime on WTTO Channel 21, an independent TV station in Birmingham.

Scrushy called the show *Viewpoint*, and hosted it with his wife Leslie. Although the show was originally designed to discuss a variety of topics, it didn't take long for Scrushy to find his message in the word of God. Leslie Scrushy, the minister's daughter, would begin each show with a devotional message, then Richard would discuss various passages from the Bible with his guests, a selection of ministers and bishops from a variety of Birmingham churches.

Scrushy's critics, including plaintiffs lawyers who were suing him on behalf of defrauded investors, accused him of trying to portray himself as a devout religious man in a program that was likely to be seen by at least some potential jurors in his trial. But a spokesman for Scrushy insisted that the former HealthSouth CEO was "raised in a churchgoing family and saved at age 11. He felt called to the ministry at age 15 but put that call aside when he moved into teaching and then business."

A frequent guest on the show, Bishop Dusty Hammock of Point of Grace Ministries, told *USA Today* that he didn't want to pass judgment on anything Scrushy may have done at HealthSouth. "Here's the way I look at it," he said. "Jesus did not say, 'I will hang out with these people, and I will not hang out with those people.' For Him, it was not a matter of guilt or innocence. My interest is in Richard Scrushy as a person. My relationship with him has nothing to do with his innocence or guilt. I feel like I'm trying to honor that."

Chapter Seven

Stock analysts

In the fall of 1999, Jack Grubman had a problem. He was making $25 million as a top research analyst at Salomon Smith Barney, but he couldn't get his kids into the right nursery school in Manhattan.

In any other part of the USA, a millionaire like Grubman would have no problem gaining his kids acceptance into an exclusive, private pre-school. But in the topsy-turvy world of private schools in Manhattan--an island filled with wealthy people who don't want to entrust their kids to the public school system--it takes more than just money to gain entrée into the city's pre-eminent pre-schools. It takes influence.

Grubman, perhaps the most famous research analyst on Wall Street, figured out a solution to his problem. One of the top executives at Citigroup, the parent company of Salomon Smith Barney, had recently asked him for a favor, and in the fall of 1999, just as Grubman was about to deliver on that favor, he decided to ask that executive for something in return.

Sanford "Sandy" Weill, one of two co-CEOs of the banking giant Citigroup, was a member of the board of directors at

AT&T. Weill's relationship with AT&T chief Michael Armstrong was good, but AT&T nevertheless shut Citigroup out of its financing deals. Investment bankers at Citigroup's Salomon Smith Barney unit were snubbed because of Grubman's negative view of Ma Bell's business prospects. Things got so bad that in the fall of 1998, in a speech about the future of the telecommunications industry, Grubman identified the companies he felt were poised to become top players in a world wired together by the Internet. He didn't mention AT&T at all.

Shortly after that speech, Grubman received a note from Weill, asking him to take a "fresh look" at AT&T. The request from Weill to Grubman was unusual. Grubman, despite his gargantuan paycheck, was not a senior executive whose job called for him to be in direct contact with Weill. It was as if President Bush had called up a CIA analyst directly and asked him to take a "fresh look" at an intelligence report stating that Iraq had no weapons of mass destruction. The CIA analyst would understand immediately what the president wanted.

Grubman interpreted the letter as a request for him to issue a positive report on the giant telecommunications company. Since AT&T CEO Mike Armstrong served on Citigroup's board of directors, such a report could bolster Weill internally in his competition with co-CEO John Reed for the top job. As an added benefit, a positive report from Grubman would also open the door at AT&T to Salomon Smith Barney's investment bankers, who had been frozen out of Ma Bell's financing activities.

Over the course of the next year, Grubman met with various executives at AT&T. He even traveled with Weill to AT&T's

New Jersey headquarters to sit down with Armstrong, the CEO. By November of 1999, he was putting the finishing touches on his new report about AT&T. In a letter Grubman wrote to Weill about his progress on the AT&T project, he asked his favor: "On another matter, as I alluded to you to the other day, we are going through the ridiculous but necessary process of pre-school applications in Manhattan. For someone who grew up in a household with a father making $8,000 a year and for someone who attended public schools, I do find this process a bit strange, but there are no bounds for what you do for your children."

After stating his wish for his twins to attend the 92nd Street Y, Grubman wrote: "Given that it's statistically easier to get into the Harvard freshman class than it is to get into pre-school at the 92nd Street Y (by the way, this is a correct statement), it comes down to 'who you know.'"

Grubman spoke to Weill six times that month about the "fresh look" at AT&T, an unprecedented amount of contact between the pair. On Nov. 30, Grubman upgraded his rating on AT&T stock from "neutral" to "buy." Over a four-year period, during which he favored upstarts like WorldCom over Ma Bell, this was the first positive report Grubman issued on AT&T.

In Feb. of 2000, AT&T responded by naming Citigroup's Salomon Smith Barney unit as the lead underwriter for the initial public offering (IPO) of its wireless division. The deal would generate $63 million in fees for Salomon Smith Barney, and to outside observers, it seemed obvious that AT&T was responding favorably to the company in return for Grubman's positive research report.

Of more interest to Grubman personally, Sandy Weill contacted a board member of the 92nd Street Y and asked that Grubman's children be given full consideration for admission. According to an investigation by the New York state Attorney General's office, the 92nd Street Y board member understood that if Grubman's children were admitted, the school could expect a hefty contribution from Weill on behalf of Citigroup. After the children were admitted, Weill agreed to donate $1 million to the school over a period of five years.

Following his upgrade of AT&T, Grubman told a subordinate and an institutional investor that he changed his view on the stock to get his children into the 92nd Street Y. A few months after AT&T completed the IPO of its wireless division, Grubman reverted to his "neutral" rating on the stock. By then, Weill had also edged out Reed to become Citigroup's sole CEO.

A year later, in an email to a friend, Carol Cutler, Grubman explained the reason for his temporary upgrade of AT&T's stock: "You know everyone thinks I upgraded T [AT&T] to get lead for AWE [AT&T's wireless spinoff]. Nope. I used Sandy to get my kids in 92nd Street Y pre-school (which is harder than Harvard) and Sandy needed Armstrong's vote on our board to nuke Reed in showdown. Once coast was clear for both of us (ie Sandy clear victor and my kids confirmed) I went back to my normal negative self on T. Armstrong never knew that we both (Sandy and I) played him like a fiddle."

Conflicts of interest

When you want to buy a new car, you do research before making a decision. If you're like most people, you talk to friends who have recently bought new cars, and you scan the automotive reviews in your local newspaper. Before you spend thousands of dollars, you want an honest, unbiased opinion about a car's strengths and weaknesses.

But when it comes to buying stocks, the game is different. You may not want to trust the advice of a friend, unless he or she studies stocks for a living. If you want independent research, done by financial experts, it costs money. The solution for many investors in the 1990s was to rely on research supplied for free from their brokerage firm.

In retrospect, it's obvious that relying on stock research from a brokerage firm would be like relying on "independent" research funded by General Motors, Ford or Toyota when buying a new car. But for much of the 1990s, despite consistent warning signals that the "independent research" supplied by brokerage firms had been compromised by the needs of those firms to generate investment banking fees from the companies they covered, investors still trusted the "free" advice of stock research analysts.

So when Jack Grubman of Salomon Smith Barney upgraded his opinion of AT&T in November of 1999, some investors bought the stock. Little did they realize that Grubman was acting, in part, to get his kids into an exclusive Manhattan preschool, and to generate tens of millions of dollars in investment banking fees for Citigroup.

It wasn't always this way. Back in 1959, three young Harvard MBAs started Wall Street's first brokerage firm dedicated to stock research and analysis. The three--William "Bill" Donaldson, Dan Lufkin and Dick Jenrette--thought that by studying a company's business closely, they could determine whether an investor should buy stock in that company.

Donaldson, Lufkin & Jenrette helped investors make smart stock picks by providing in-depth research. Investors--mostly large institutions which bought a stake in a company for the long haul--rewarded DLJ for its insights by placing orders to buy those big chunks of stock through the brokerage firm. DLJ made its money on the fixed commissions from those purchases.

Donaldson, Lufkin & Jenrette blazed a new path in stock research. Before 1959, investors had to research companies on their own. Brokerage houses such as Merrill Lynchsupplied market information and statistical analyses to their customers, but DLJ approached the job differently, providing investors with a sophisticated analysis of a company's operations, including its competitive advantages over rivals and future prospects. The approach, according to Donaldson, was to analyze a company the same way a management consulting firm such as McKinsey would.

Over the next decade, other Wall Street brokerage firms, trying to mimic DLJ's success, started their own research departments. In 1970, DLJ itself went public.

The end of an era

In 1975, the "golden age of Wall Street research" came to an end when Congress passed legislation forcing brokerage firms to compete on the commissions they charged to buy and sell stocks for investors. These days, investors pay miniscule sums of money to trade stocks, with some online stock trading services charging commissions of just 5 cents per share. Prior to 1975, trading costs were closer to 75 cents per share.

The end of the fixed commission system doomed quality research in two ways. First, the change allowed discount brokers to strip away trades from established firms like DLJ, Merrill Lynch and others. As discount brokerage firms cut into the revenue that brokerage houses made from commissions, those firms had less money to spend on research.

The other major change generated by the end of fixed commission rates was a transformation of investor behavior. When the cost of trading stocks was high, investors were reluctant to move in and out of positions, since the churn would drive up their costs. Instead, pre-1975 investors thought long range. This investment strategy, sometimes referred to as "value investing," is the method preferred by Warren Buffett, the fabled stock picker and head of Berkshire Hathaway.

After 1975, a new class of investors was born: short-term "market timers." These investors, including what became known as "day traders," didn't care about a company's fundamental strengths or weaknesses. Instead, they cared what *other investors* thought of the stock, and tried to profit accordingly. If they thought other investors would bid the stock up, these short-term investors wanted to be in.

In some ways, the Great Bull market that began in 1982 and lasted until 2000 was driven by the ease with which investors could buy and sell stocks. Low transaction costs helped attract new investors, including millions of Americans who poured their money into mutual funds, and others who started investing in individual stocks for the first time. This infusion of new money in the 1980s and 1990s helped drive the price of stocks up across the board. But the seemingly unstoppable rise of the Dow Jones Industrial Average did not improve the quality of stock research.

Research analysts were reluctant to issue reports advising clients to sell a particular stock. Many analysts abided by the saying, "if you can't say something good, don't bother saying anything at all." That sentiment was reinforced in March 1990 when Marvin Roffman, an analyst in the Philadelphia office of Janney Montgomery Scott, predicted that Donald Trump's new Taj Mahal casino in Atlantic City would lose money. Trump complained to the firm and Roffman was fired. The message to research analysts on Wall Street was clear: if you spoke ill of a stock, even if you were right, you were putting your career in jeopardy.

By the 1990s, major brokerage firms realized that they couldn't survive and prosper simply by selling stocks to investors. The big money was in investment banking: helping private companies issue stock to the public for the first time; or helping public companies arrange additional financing through the issuance of new shares of stock, or bonds. And so began a wave of consolidation: Morgan Stanley merged with Dean Witter; Salomon Brothers acquired Smith Barney. As these companies came together, their top executives saw that the "free" stock research they were supplying to investors was a drag on profits. Research analysts existed to help the brokerage firms sell stocks to investors. But if these newly merged financial giants could get the analysts to work more closely with the investment bankers, they could reap enormous profits.

Stock market regulators had always been concerned about the possibility that a brokerage firm would use a research analyst to drum up banking business. Therefore, over time these brokerage firms swore to keep the researchers separate from the rainmakers in investment banking. They pledged to put a "Chinese Wall" between the two groups.

In the 1990s, with the boom in technology stocks and the rise of the Internet, brokerage houses saw big financial opportunities in taking dot-com start-up companies public. Increasingly, as these firms "pitched" technology companies to award them their IPO assignments, the investment bankers brought along research analysts who promised to provide "coverage" of the start-ups.

By promising "coverage," a stock analyst guaranteed that he or she would write regularly about the company, which in itself was a plus. The vast majority of 14,000 publicly traded companies in the U.S. do not have analysts tracking their earnings and operations. Executives at firms that were going public realized that having one or several analysts follow their stock would boost buying interest among investors.

The most extreme examples of the marriage between research analysts and investment bankers occurred at Salomon Smith Barney, where Jack Grubman established himself as Wall Street's pre-eminent telecommunications analyst, and Morgan Stanley, where Mary Meeker was so enthusiastic about Internet companies that she became known as the "Queen of the 'Net.' "

Jack Grubman's revolution

A mathematics major who worked at AT&T before becoming a stock analyst in 1985, Grubman was an unlikely candidate to become the poster boy for the decline and fall of independent research. Prior to the Internet boom, telecommunications was an interesting, but unglamorous industry. Ma Bell was broken up into the "Baby Bells," and MCI and Sprint began taking market share away from AT&T, but the industry was less appealing to investors than the burgeoning high-technology category, which flourished with the advent of the personal computer.

But as more and more people bought computers and went online in the 1990s, technology executives realized that a wired world would need millions of miles of fiber optic cables to allow everyone to surf the web when they wanted. New telecommunications companies sprang up, and investors looked to industry experts like Grubman to guide them.

Grubman's reputation as a telecommunications guru grew to the point where he became more than an outside observer of the industry--he became a player himself. In October of 1996, during a visit in Denver with Philip Anschutz, the founder of Qwest Communications, Grubman promised the billionaire investor that he could get a top AT&T executive to jump ship and take the job as Qwest's CEO.

Sure enough, a few months later, Joe Nacchio left his job as head of AT&T's bread-and-butter division, long distance calling, to become CEO of the obscure start-up. Nacchio's willingness to leave one of the most powerful positions in the industry for Qwest bestowed immediate credibility on the Denver telecom firm and enhanced Grubman's reputation as a power broker. But it also ended Grubman's ability to render a detached opinion of Qwest's prospects. He would never be able to criticize the company's performance or cut back his opinion on Qwest's stock. How could he? After all, he had selected the CEO!

In the late 1990s, Grubman's direct involvement with the top executives of upstart telecommunications companies appeared to be a "win-win." Grubman met with executives such as WorldCom CEO Bernie Ebbers, gave those CEOs advice on how to run their companies and issued bullish research reports on their firms. In a stock market obsessed with the limitless growth potential of the Internet (the stock prices of Amazon and other online companies surged to ridiculous heights, even when these companies were losing money), telecommunications companies could do no wrong, since they would be laying down the fiber optic cable designed to connect online users with each other. Grubman's bullish recommendations of these companies paid off for investors who followed his advice: the stocks of WorldCom, Qwest, Global Crossing and other telecom start-ups rose at a much steeper rate than the stock of sleepy old AT&T.

In this climate, it seemed as though the old rule that research analysts should be independent and skeptical of the companies they followed was quaint, even naïve. Grubman told *BusinessWeek* in 2000 that "what used to be a conflict is now synergy." He added: "Someone like me who is banking-intensive would have been looked at disdainfully by the buy side 15 years ago. Now they know that I'm in the flow of what's going on. That helps me help them think about the industry." On the subject of objectivity, which used to be a hallmark for research analysts, Grubman was dismissive: "Objective? The other word for it is uninformed."

Judgment day

Just as the success of DLJ some 40 years earlier spawned numerous imitators, the rise of Grubman and Meeker to the top ranks of research analysts, making millions of dollars per year, transformed the industry. By the late 1990s, all the major brokerage firms encouraged their analysts to become "stars," either by appearing on financial news programs, particularly those on CNBC, or being quoted in news articles.

One young analyst became a star with his bullish forecast of Amazon's stock price in December of 1998. Henry Blodget was an analyst at CIBC Oppenheimer when Amazon stock, swelling amid a frenzy of Internet hype, soared to $250 per share. Jonathan Cohen, the Merrill Lynch analyst responsible for Internet stocks, warned investors that Amazon was over-priced and probably not worth more than $50 per share, but Blodget, a relatively unknown analyst, said the stock could rise as high as $400 per share over the next 12 months.

What happened next defined the erratic nature of the Internet bubble. Based on Blodget's optimistic forecast, frenzied investors bid up Amazon's stock almost 20%. Sure enough, the buying momentum behind Amazon stock propelled it past the $400 mark in just one month, and Merrill Lynch hired Blodget to be its Internet stock analyst, replacing Cohen, who decided to leave the business altogether. Blodget eventually earned an annual salary of $12 million at Merrill, and his group worked closely with Merrill's investment bankers to help the firm convince a wave of dot-com start-ups that they should hire the firm to manage their IPOs.

The transformation of the 33-year-old Blodget from an obscure booster of Internet stocks at a second-tier brokerage firm to the top dot-com analyst at Merrill Lynch showed that the market for stock research had ceased having anything to do with long-term analysis of a company's fundamental business operations and everything to do with accurately predicting whether other people were going to buy or sell the stock in the short term.

Of course, a stock market can't keep going up simply because everybody thinks it's going to go up. At some point, a stock's price has to reflect what people realistically think the company's business potential is. In the spring of 2000, investor sentiment changed. Institutional investors that had enjoyed the long ride up in stock prices grew concerned that the inflated prices of technology stocks wouldn't last, so they began to sell.

Seeing the big players sell, other investors followed suit, and through much of 2000, investors of all kinds dumped stock shares, particularly the stocks of Internet companies, which began to fail. Just as they had stampeded like bulls in the late 1990s, driving prices upwards, investors stampeded in the other direction in 2000, selling the stocks of Internet companies and technology companies.

Some investors sued their brokerage firms, claiming that they had poured their savings into fly-by-night Internet stocks because analysts like Blodget recommended them. In 2001, Debases Kanjilal, a doctor in Queens, N.Y., sued Merrill Lynch, claiming that he lost almost half a million dollars by investing in InfoSpace, a dot-com start-up, on Blodget's recommendation. As the stock price sank from $122 per share down to less than $10, Kanjilal claimed that he tried to sell the stock, only to be told by Merrill Lynch brokers that he should hold on to it, because Blodget was predicting growth for the company. Merrill eventually reached an out-of-court settlement with Kanjilal.

Kanjalil's lawsuit against Merrill attracted the attention of Eliot Spitzer, the Attorney General of New York, who launched an investigation into Blodget's research practices. Although federal securities laws are enforced by the Securities and Exchange Commission, a New York law called the Martin Act gave Spitzer the authority to investigate the activities of Wall Street stock analysts. The Martin Act, among other things, forbids any company that sells stock from engaging in deceptive sales practices.

Spitzer's investigators found a stream of emails from Blodget to his subordinates that seemed to confirm his suspicions: that Blodget gave aggressive "buy" ratings to companies that did banking business with Merrill Lynch. In one case, Blodget referred to the stock of a company he was recommending as a "dog"; in another, he referred to a stock touted by Merrill Lynch as a "piece of shit."

The most damning email uncovered by Spitzer's team concerned a company called Internet Capital Group, which Merrill Lynch had taken public in 1999. Some of Merrill Lynch's local managers across the USA, who recommended stocks to mom-and-pop investors based on Blodget's forecasts, complained bitterly about how their clients were losing large sums of money by following the firm's advice. Fed up with the complaints from the field, Blodget fired off an email of his own, saying: "The more I read of these, the less willing I am to cut companies any slack, regardless of the predictable temper tantrums, threats, and/or relationship damage that are likely to follow."

Using this email as proof that the quality of Merrill Lynch's research was distorted by the brokerage firm's relationship with a banking client, Spitzer threatened legal action. Merrill Lynch settled with New York State, vowing to keep its research separate from its investment banking practices, and agreeing to pay a fine of $100 million.

After the Merrill Lynch settlement, Spitzer, along with regulators from other states, delved into the research practices of all the big financial services firms. That's when Spitzer's investigators discovered the emails from Grubman at Salomon Smith Barney indicating that the analyst had changed his outlook on AT&T from "neutral" to "buy" in the hope that Citigroup CEO Sandy Weill would help him get his kids accepted into the exclusive 92nd Street Y pre-school.

In all, state investigators and SEC regulators uncovered similar research abuses at 10 major Wall Street firms. In April of 2003, after months of haggling, the 10 firms entered into a "global settlement" with all of the regulators, calling for a grand payment of $1.4 billion (some of which would go into an investor compensation fund) and promises that in the future, analysts would not participate in investment banking deals.

SEC chairman William Donaldson, who had founded DLJ more than four decades earlier, declared: "Our unified action brings to a close a period during which the once-respected research profession became nearly unrecognizable to earlier generations of investors and analysts. As many of you know, I helped found an investment firm that bore my name and which was originally dedicated to research. For that reason, I speak very personally, when I say that I am profoundly saddened - and angry - about the conduct that's alleged in our complaints. There is absolutely no place for it in our markets and it cannot be tolerated. When an analyst signs his or her name, and places the firm's name, on a research report expressing strong support for an issuer, while admitting privately to doubts about the company's viability, the only appropriate reaction is outrage."

Blodget entered into a separate settlement with the SEC and Spitzer, agreeing to a lifetime ban from the securities industry and paying a fine of $4 million. Grubman, too, was banned from the securities industry, and paid $15 million fine. He could afford it, since Citigroup had given him $32 in severance upon his departure from Salomon Smith Barney in 2002.

As for his children, they finished nursery school at the 92nd Street Y, but because of the notoriety brought on by the disclosure of how they got in, the two were denied admission to Manhattan's elite private grammar schools.

Chapter Eight

The Securities Cops

On a Sunday evening in February of 2003, Peter Scannell sat in his Volvo near a church in Quincy, Mass., sipping coffee, listening to the radio, and killing time before an Alcoholics Anonymous meeting. The weather was sleeting outside, so Scannell stayed in, window rolled up.

Suddenly, his door flew open. Scannell looked up and saw what he later described as a "big, burly man with a full beard." The stranger yanked Scannell partially out of the car and bashed him on the head with a brick several times, until he lost consciousness. Nearly an hour later, a police officer arrived and found Scannell slumped over, a gash in the back of his head, held in the car by his shoulder belt.

After regaining consciousness, Scannell pieced together what had happened. For the previous three years, he had worked at the Quincy call center of a prominent Boston-based mutual fund, Putnam Investments. Over that time, he had noticed a disturbing trend: members of two unions--representing electricians and boilermakers--used to call him regularly and shift their entire retirement accounts from one fund to another, and back again a day later.

Scannell soon realized that the union members were engaged in a practice known as "market timing," which most mutual fund companies aren't supposed to allow. Members of the boilermakers, based in New York, seemed to have found a foolproof way to make money: each afternoon, they would phone in to Putnam's call center, and if the overall stock market was up for the day, they'd transfer all of their holdings into an international fund. If the market was down, they'd shift all of their money back into a domestic fund.

This system worked because most mutual funds set their prices once a day, at the close of trading. But international funds react, in part, to market conditions in the USA. So if the domestic stock market is up, most international funds--which set their prices overnight--would see a rise when the market opened in Europe or Japan.

By shifting quickly from one day to the next, the boilermakers were thus able to guarantee themselves an automatic profit of a few pennies per share. When the U.S. market was good, they would sell at a price that had just been jacked up a few cents at 4 p.m. Then they would buy the international fund, confident that it would rise the following day in the wake of the strong showing in the U.S. market. When domestic stocks dropped, the boilermakers would reverse direction, cashing out of their international funds before what would certainly be a down day, and buying U.S. funds at a recently lowered price.

On a day-by-day basis, the profits weren't big. But over the course of three years, Scannell calculated that it could be a lucrative game. Scannell tracked the trades of 10 boilermakers over a two-and-a-half-year period, and found that they made

5,340 trades involving $657 million in assets. The net profit: $2 million. Scannell calculated that one boilermaker made 542 trades in that period, boosting his holdings from $525,000 to $1,472,000, a gain of $947,000.

Mutual funds aren't supposed to allow market-timing trades because the individual market timer profits at the expense of long-term shareholders. By darting in and out of funds, the boilermakers raised the costs those funds incurred, costs which were passed on to regular investors. The market timers also forced the fund managers to keep a larger amount of cash on hand (instead of invested in stocks) in order to pay for their frequent trips out. In short, the boilermakers' profits hurt other Putnam investors.

That's what bothered Scannell.

He alerted some of Putnam's managers to what was going on, but says they weren't interested in halting the practice. Fed up with their attitude, on Jan. 30, 2003, Scannell told his bosses he wasn't going to accept market-timing trades anymore. Fearing for his job, he took a trove of Putnam trading documents home with him that evening. In a report he later filed with regulators, Scannell wrote, "I drove home looking over my shoulder. I remember laughing at how paranoid I was--actually I was shaking, I was so scared."

It was just a few days later, parked in an alley outside the Quincy church, that Scannell was attacked. His assailant--the big, bearded man--wore a New York Yankees baseball cap and a gray sweatshirt that said "Boilermakers Local 5" across the chest. The man threatened Scannell about the waves he was making at Putnam and told him to keep quiet about it. Scannell couldn't believe that someone from the boilermakers union had attacked him--the baseball cap and the sweatshirt were too obvious. But he didn't know what to do.

After about two months, he decided to blow the whistle on his employer. In April, accompanied by a lawyer, he went to the Boston office of the Securities and Exchange Commission, the financial "police force" charged with enforcing the nation's securities laws, and told them what he had witnessed at Putnam. He provided three SEC lawyers with spreadsheets showing the market-timing activity and e-mails from his managers. At the end of the hour-long meeting with Scannell, the SEC lawyers thanked him for his "courage," and told him they would handle it the matter.

But months went by, and the SEC seemed to do nothing. When Scannell called the SEC's Boston office, he was informed that any investigation into Putnam was private. By September, he could wait no longer, and decided to tell his story to Massachusetts state regulators. William Galvin, the Secretary of State, moved quickly on Scannell's complaint, issuing a subpoena to Putnam on the day of his agency's meeting with Scannell, demanding a long list of trading records.

Galvin's office confirmed that what Scannell was complaining about was true. Worse, state regulators and the SEC discovered that six of Putnam's own executives engaged in similar market-timing practices that padded the earnings of their own mutual fund holdings, but hurt those of the average investor. Putnam CEO Larry Lasser, one of the best-paid executives in the industry, was forced to resign.

The SEC demanded that Putnam correct the market-timing abuses, and in April of 2004, the federal agency and

Massachusetts regulators hit the mutual fund firm with a $110 million fine. But Scannell's role in unraveling the misbehavior at Putnam, and the SEC's sluggishness in following up his tip, exposed a huge problem at the agency charged with protecting the nation's investors.

In 2002 and 2003, state regulators such as Galvin and New York Attorney General Eliot Spitzer had been quietly grousing about the SEC's inability to police the securities industry. After the Putnam scandal was exposed, they criticized the agency openly.

"Heads should roll at the SEC," Spitzer complained in an interview with *The New York Times.* "There is a whole division at the SEC that is supposed to be looking at mutual funds. Where have they been?" Shortly after Massachusetts and the SEC announced their findings about Putnam, the head of the SEC's Boston office resigned, a concession to public pressure that was extraordinary in a federal agency where no one ever got fired.

The Keystone Kops

Spitzer's charge against the SEC stung because it was true. Ever since Enron shocked investors and the public by deflating like a balloon late in 2001, it was obvious that the federal agency charged with policing the securities industry was overwhelmed by its duties. Just as politicians and the public, in the wake of the Sept. 11 attacks, demanded to know why the FBI and the CIA weren't able to prevent terrorists from hijacking planes and crashing them into buildings, after Enron's collapse, public officials demanded to know what the SEC had been doing to prevent financial catastrophes.

What the public learned wasn't pretty: for almost a decade, during the greatest surge in the history of the U.S. stock market, the SEC had been transformed from a lean but efficient police force patrolling the securities industry into the Keystone Kops. In the 1980s, at the height of another boom market, the SEC helped puncture a massive insider trading scandal on Wall Street headed by Ivan Boesky. Working with the SEC, ambitious federal prosecutors in Manhattan, led by Rudolph Giuliani, secured guilty pleas from Boesky and his biggest patron, junk bond king Michael Milken.

By 2002, in the wake of Enron's collapse and the exposure of a multi-billion-dollar accounting fraud at WorldCom, the SEC's role in apprehending big-league cheaters like Boesky was a distant memory. Instead, at the end of a decade of booming growth, auditors, executives at public companies and their lawyers felt little fear of the securities cops.

No respect

In 2001, a former employee of Computer Associates tipped off the SEC about shady accounting practices at the business software company. Computer Associates had already attracted the SEC's notice in 2000 when it changed the way it recorded revenues from sales, allowing it to jack up its numbers quickly. Such accounting changes raise suspicions at the SEC, especially when their primary goal seems to be to make the company's sales figures look better.

But the tips that came into the SEC caused more concern. According to several former Computer Associates salespeople, the company had created a new measurement of time not found on any calendar: the "35-day month." The former sales representatives told the SEC that Computer Associates finance and accounting personnel would sometimes hold the monthly books open at the end of a quarter for an extra week or so, in order to claim more sales that could be booked in the previous quarter, a gross violation of securities laws.

In early 2002, the SEC launched a formal investigation of the company. Computer Associates hired a respected Manhattan law firm, and told investigators that the company would cooperate fully with the investigation. But that's not what happened. Instead, some of the company's top executives, including chief financial officer Ira Zar, did everything they could to thwart the SEC investigation.

First off, Zar and his colleagues lied to the law firm they'd just hired, insisting that there was no truth to the allegations of a "35-day month." Because of those lies, Computer Associates' law firm unwittingly started feeding misinformation to the SEC. When investigators wanted to interview one of the company's finance executives, Zar and his colleagues pressured that executive into denying the existence of the "35-day month." At Zar's request, an executive named Lloyd Silverstein told the SEC a cover story about how Computer Associates accounted for its sales revenue. In January of 2004, Silverstein pleaded guilty to obstructing the SEC's investigation. Three months later, Zar and two of his colleagues also entered guilty pleas with the U.S. Attorney in Brooklyn, N.Y.

Even Martha Stewart had no respect for the SEC. As described in Chapter One, ImClone CEO Sam Waksal knew on Dec. 27, 2001, that an adverse ruling from the FDA was about to drive his company's stock price down. So he tried to unload stock in his company. Waksal's Merrill Lynch broker, Peter Bacanovic, was on vacation in Florida, but he realized that if Waksal was trying to sell his shares, something bad was about to happen to the stock. Bacanovic immediately thought of one of his other clients, Martha Stewart.

Although it was against Merrill Lynch's rules, Bacanovic tried to pass the sensitive information on to Stewart. But since he was in Florida, and Stewart was enroute to Mexico for her own vacation, Bacanovic left a message at Stewart's office for her to call his office at Merrill Lynch. Then he gave his assistant, Douglas Faneuil, specific directions to inform Stewart about Waksal's attempts to sell. Faneuil, a newcomer to Merrill Lynch, asked Bacanovic if it was alright to share that kind of information with Stewart. "You must. You've got to, that's the whole point," Bacanovic told him.

Around 1:30 on the afternoon of Dec. 27, 2001, Stewart's private jet landed at an airport near San Antonio to refuel. The super-star businesswoman, who owned the majority of stock in her own publicly traded company, Martha Stewart Living Omnimedia, called her office to speak to some of her employees and check her messages. She learned that Bacanovic had called and left a message, saying he believed that ImClone stock was "going to start trading downward."

Stewart called Bacanovic's office and the 26-year-old Faneuil picked up the phone. Stewart asked what was going on with Waksal, and Faneuil told her that Waksal was trying to sell his stock. All of his ImClone stock? Stewart asked. Just the shares that Waksal held at Merrill Lynch, Faneuil replied. Stewart asked Faneuil what the price of ImClone stock was at that moment. Told that it was trading in the $59 range, Stewart ordered the broker's assistant to sell her entire stake of 3,928 shares, for a total of $229,500.

The next day, Dec. 28, the FDA announced its negative decision regarding Erbitux, ImClone's cancer drug. As expected, the company's share price dropped steeply. By the end of the next trading day, it had dropped 16%, plunging to $47 per share. If Stewart had sold then, after investors learned of the FDA announcement, she would have received only $184,000 for her ImClone stock. Bacanovic's tip thus resulted in a $45,000 gain for a woman who was worth almost $1 billion at the time.

Internal investigators at Merrill Lynch, as well as SEC lawyers, learned quickly of Waksal's attempts to sell his ImClone shares. The SEC interviewed him, but Waksal lied. At the same time, the SEC also learned about Stewart's sale of ImClone stock. Agency investigators suspected that Stewart might have been tipped off about the FDA news. But in an interview with the SEC in February of 2002, Stewart denied that she had any inside information about ImClone. She was asked if she had spoken to Waksal that day and said she hadn't. She said she sold her stock because she and her broker, Bacanovic, had an agreement that if ImClone stock dropped below $60 per share, they would sell.

But Stewart's answers didn't satisfy the SEC lawyers or the federal prosecutor who conducted the interview. When they subsequently learned that Stewart had placed a call to Waksal's office immediately after selling her stock, they grew more suspicious and conducted a second interview, this one over the phone. Stewart again lied about the reason for her sale, sticking with her story about the $60 agreement.

Bacanovic lied to SEC lawyers as well. In a recorded interview, he was asked if he let Stewart know about Sam Waksal's desperate attempts to sell his ImClone stock. He denied doing any such thing, explaining that it was against Merrill Lynch policy to violate confidentialities like client trading patterns. For a few months, Faneuil went along with his boss' story, but his conscience bothered him. In June of 2002, he confessed to prosecutors and SEC lawyers that the whole $60 agreement was a cover-up designed to hide the real reason for Stewart's stock sale.

The U.S. Attorney in Manhattan eventually charged Stewart and Bacanovic with making false statements and obstructing an SEC investigation. In March of 2004, following a six-week trial, a panel of 12 jurors convicted the pair.

The verdict against Stewart and Bacanovic appalled many of the domestic diva's most ardent supporters, who thought the government was picking on her because she was a successful woman. But for defense lawyers who represent corporate executives before the SEC, it was a huge boost. Until Stewart's conviction, many executives looked down on the SEC as an ineffectual, pestering agency that was to be tolerated, but never feared.

The prime reason for this disdainful attitude is that the SEC's legal powers extend only to civil, and not criminal, enforcement actions. Civil actions can be a threat to auditing firms, stock brokerage houses and mutual fund companies, all of which need to be registered with the SEC to conduct their business. But to high-powered executives like Stewart, the SEC was more of an annoyance. Securities lawyers across the USA, especially those who work at big corporate law firms, say that the single biggest challenge they face when representing a client before the SEC is to determine whether that client is telling *them* the truth.

Days after the Martha Stewart verdict, one former SEC enforcement attorney told *USA Today*, "It's cheering to find that there are consequences to lying to SEC, which is widely considered to be a popular indoor sport in the United States. Whether this is something that portends a new attitude, or is a one-time symbolic gesture remains to be seen."

The starving of the SEC

Not long after President Bill Clinton named Arthur Levitt to be chairman of the SEC in 1993, Levitt realized that for the SEC to be an effective police force of the stock market, it would need enough money to pay its professionals good salaries, and to hire young talent for the long term. In addition, while the world of stock brokerages and public companies was becoming increasingly wired--with stocks being traded by investors working on computers--the SEC would need a massive investment in technology to help it keep up with the challenge of a booming stock market.

Each year at budget time, the chairman of the SEC would have to approach key members of Congress--the ones whose committees held the power of the purse over the SEC--and beg for increases in funding. By design, the process keeps the SEC beholden to various Representatives and Senators. But Levitt wanted to change that. After being sworn in as SEC chairman, Levitt proposed that the SEC be funded with the money it collected through public company filings. Each year, the SEC collects hundreds of millions of dollars from registered companies and turns that money over to the U.S. Treasury. If it could only keep that money--at no direct cost to the U.S. taxpayer--the commission would be able to pay for a top-flight securities police force.

In 1993, for example, the SEC collected $517 million in fees, but Congress budgeted only $253 million for the commission. By 2001, the SEC collected $2 billion, more than five times the commission's $382 million budget for that year. But self-funding was not to be. The House of Representatives approved the idea in 1993, but several Senators fought the concept, and it never made it into law.

In his memoir, *Take on the Street,* Levitt admits that the idea of self-funding for the SEC was "naïve." In Washington, a Representative's or Senator's power is directly tied to how much authority he or she has over key federal agencies and programs. Lawmakers who have the power of the purse over the SEC generate campaign contributions from financial institutions who want to have some sway over the commission. If Congress gave up its funding control over the SEC, there would be no reason for the USA's biggest banks, brokerage houses and accounting firms to shovel hefty sums of money to the election campaigns of the commission's overseers.

Besides, after the Republicans swept control of both houses of Congress in 1994, legislators were more interested in reducing regulations in the financial markets than in funding increased regulation. According to Joel Seligman's comprehensive history of the SEC, *The Transformation of Wall Street,* the Republican Congress wanted to scale back the SEC's power. "By the summer of 1995," Seligman writes, "new legislation had been introduced to redefine the Commission's mission, freeze the SEC budget for five years, and reduce the number of SEC commissioners from five to three."

That legislation went nowhere, but the message was clear: the Republican-controlled Congress would be tight-fisted with the SEC, and aggressive about keeping the commission on a tight leash. From 1989 to 1993, during the administration of the first President Bush, the SEC's budget grew 19% per year, and staff positions increased by 4.6% each year. But during Levitt's eight years at the SEC's helm, Congress would never be so generous. From 1993 to 2000, the budget grew an average of 6% per year, and staff positions increased by only 1.4% annually.

The fundamental premise behind the SEC--that it existed to protect the average investor--was being challenged by a group of lawmakers (including some Democrats), who felt that the commission's regulations hampered business growth. And when Congress passed the Private Securities Litigation Reform Act in 1995, accounting firms no longer feared getting sued after a blown audit. Suddenly, the deck was stacked against the Main Street investor.

Stagnation

In corporate America, businesses that don't grow tend to stagnate and die. Once Congress restricted its funding, the SEC began to drift. When a corporation loses its way, its best employees leave for better jobs and salaries elsewhere. The same principle holds true for government agencies. When Congress responded to a booming stock market by restricting the SEC's budget, life got worse for the commission's lawyers and accountants. Their hours got longer and their work became more frustrating. No fat bonuses or salary spikes for them.

The best of these lawyers and accountants knew they could double their salaries by leaving the commission for the private sector. Thus began a massive exodus of talent from the commission in the late 1990s, at the very time when the SEC could

least afford it. As many of its most experienced officials departed, the commission had to rely heavily on junior staffers who
needed on-the-job training before they would become effective.

The commission's low point came in the period between 1998
and 2000. During those years, as the Dow Jones Industrial
Average and Nasdaq markets were vaulting to all-time highs,
more than 1,000 employees--one-third of the SEC's staff--left. A
Congressional study of the exodus showed that most of these
lawyers and accountants bolted because of the low pay, especially when compared to the salaries earned by bank regulators. But the departees also complained about the lack of opportunity for promotion within the SEC, and the lack of administrative support.

At most law firms, partners rely on junior lawyers to do the
time-consuming grunt work like writing and filing motionsin
court. At the SEC, there is virtually no administrative support:
senior lawyers get bogged down in tedious chores that should
be delegated.

Congressional leaders inflicted pain on the SEC in other ways,
too. After 1994, lawmakers used their positions to lord it over
the commission. When an SEC ruling affected a particular
business--forbidding it from recognizing revenue in a certain
way, for example--the CEO of that company would contact his
Representative or Senator (to whom he had contributed lots of
money) and demand action. That lawmaker would then call
one of the SEC's top officials, who was already overworked, and
demand that he or she come over to a private meeting on
Capitol Hill to explain the SEC's position.

According to Lynn Turner, former chief accountant of the SEC, those meetings were an enormous drain on SEC resources. When he was called over to the Hill, Turner couldn't just show up at the lawmaker's office for a 9 a.m. appointment and be done by 9:30. He had to prepare for each meeting by boning up on the specific issues involved, requiring several staff members to invest hours, if not days, preparing background materials. At the meeting, the lawmaker would browbeat Turner, demanding to know why an important campaign contributor did not receive a favorable ruling on some particular issue.

In the late 1990s, as the stock market boomed and businesses looked for every break they could get from the SEC, these meetings occurred with alarming frequency. The cumulative effect was to further undermine the SEC's primary mission of regulating the securities markets. "I spent a lot of time on the Hill," recalls Turner. "Any time a special interest group of constituents came into town, some Congressman, Congresswoman or Senator would call us up to the Hill for briefings. We would have to meet with them and one of their constituents. It might be a businessman who wanted to do an acquisition and do it in a way that was not allowed. You could either roll over for that Congressman, or stick to your principles and get tied up for a year. What a waste of taxpayer money!"

Cops without bullets

After the SEC successfully broke Ivan Boesky's insider trading ring in 1986, its enforcement division was feared. But just a decade later, instead of looking like marshal Wyatt Earp, SEC staffers started looking like the Texans at the Alamo or Custer at Little Big Horn.

The SEC's division of corporation finance, which reviews the filings of public companies, was swamped. With a staff of 161, the division's accountants were charged with examining the quarterly and annual earnings statements of some 14,000 publicly traded companies. They could barely plow their way through the statements of 2,000 companies, and even then, their reviews weren't thorough. But in the late 1990s, Levitt's SEC felt that the biggest risk to investors was the flood of new companies that were selling stock for the first time in initial public offerings (IPOs). Because of the higher risk involved in these new issues, Levitt committed many of the commission's accountants to this area, further removing them from the usual tasks of scouring the financial statements of Enron, WorldCom and other companies.

As the stock market soared, the SEC enforcement division's civil penalties appeared ever weaker. If the SEC found that an executive was cooking his company's books, the enforcement division could fine him $100,000 per violation for up to five violations, meaning that the maximum fine the SEC could extract from an individual executive was $500,000. As stock market frauds multiplied in the 1990s, those fines seemed laughably small.

Worse, targets of SEC investigations could always settle litigation without admitting guilt. Companies that artificially pumped up their stock prices were invariably sued by plaintiffs' lawyers seeking huge damages. Any type of admission of guilt would lead to an automatic victory for the class-action lawyers, so public companies had an incentive to fight the SEC to the bitter end. To avoid these costly legal battles, the commission got into the habit of settling cases in which the target company neither admitted nor denied wrongdoing.

The policy was an imperfect solution. It helped the SEC reach settlements in the vast majority of cases it brought, but in the long run, the policy reinforced the notion that the commission was not to be taken seriously. If an SEC investigator wanted to interview a corporate executive about accounting irregularities, that executive wouldn't worry about being grilled by Perry Mason. More likely, he'd prepare for a confrontation with Andy Mayberry and Barney Fife.

In April of 2002, at a Senate hearing into the SEC's inability to detect the fraud at Enron, Turner, the former SEC chief accountant, outlined the scope of the problems facing the commission. He testified that the SEC had 60 accountants available to work on a constant flow of 200 to 250 enforcement cases against auditing firms or their clients. Each SEC accountant would have to fly solo on three or four cases at once. But the auditing firms would assign three to four accountants to work on a single case. Translation: the SEC was outgunned.

"Simple multiplication tells one very clearly that the odds are good to excellent the SEC will not be able to successfully investigate many of the financial fraud cases in front of it," Turner said. "When confronted with a difficult case, we would sometimes have to decide whether to take a settlement we really did not like, or face the prospect of spending a disproportionate share of resources litigating it. Often litigating a case to achieve justice for investors might mean other worthy cases would have to be dropped. It was a trade-off that happened all too often for the law enforcement agency charged with overseeing the integrity of the markets." Turner added that corporate lawyers, including many who had previously worked at the SEC, "knew all too well that they could and would likely win the war of attrition."

Worse than this war of attrition, SEC enforcement officials lacked the silver bullet of criminal enforcement powers. When the SEC worked in tandem with federal prosecutors, the commission's threats of legal action carried significant weight. But the Justice Department of the 1990s showed little appetite for taking SEC civil enforcement actions and turning them into federal criminal cases.

By long-established practice, the SEC worked with prosecutors from the U.S. Attorney's office in Manhattan, just a few blocks from Wall Street. Other federal prosecutors in Brooklyn, N.Y. and in New Jersey also developed expertise in bringing securities fraud cases against corporate executives. But by and large, most prosecutors across the USA avoided such cases, because they were unglamorous, time-consuming and paper-intensive.

The collapse of Enron in 2001 sparked public outrage and resulted in a tectonic shift in the thinking of prosecutors across the country. The Justice Department made fighting securities fraud a top priority. The Enron Task Force, a posse of 25-30 seasoned prosecutors, FBI agents and IRS agents, was formed to bring criminal charges against any Enron executive implicated in the company's fraud, and any outside executive who enabled the company to commit fraud.

In July of 2002, after the fraud at WorldCom was revealed, President George W. Bush announced the creation of a "Corporate Fraud Task Force," whose job it was to blend the securities expertise of the SEC with the criminal law enforcement expertise of the FBI and the Justice Department. This presidential mandate spurred prosecutors across the country to become more active in making criminal cases out of transgressions that only a few years ago were treated as civil cases.

Congress acts

The wave of corporate accounting scandals also jolted Congress into action. In July of 2002, lawmakers passed the Sarbanes-Oxley Act, the most significant piece of securities legislation since the orginal Securities and Exchange Commission acts of 1933 and 1934.

The law closed one of the biggest loopholes that top executives used to hide from criminal liability: ignorance. Up until Sarbanes-Oxley, the CEO or chief financial officer of a company that defrauded stockholders could claim that he didn't know that the books were cooked; he could blame it on the accountants. (The accountants, in turn, would blame the corporate executives for deceiving them.)

But the Sarbanes-Oxley bill requires the top executives of a public company to be held liable for financial statements they submit to the SEC. The claim, "I didn't know about the fraud," would no longer be an effective defense against criminal prosecution. The law also stiffened criminal penalities against corporate crooks, requiring much longer jail terms for securities fraud. The public found out just how tough those new criminal penalties were in March of 2004 when Jamie Olis, a former vice president of finance at Dynegy, a Houston energy company, was convicted of fraud and sentenced to 24 years in jail. Barring a successful appeal, Olis, 38, will be in prison until he's 62.

Sarbanes-Oxley also created a new panel, the Public Company Accounting Oversight Board (PCAOB), to monitor the activities of the nation's auditing firms. The PCAOB's creation came about only because lawmakers were forced to recognize that the auditing firms which contributed so heavily to their election campaigns couldn't be trusted to regulate themselves. Along with the new rules and regulations, Sarbanes-Oxley called for a significant increase in SEC funding. The commission's budget, which had jumped to $487 million in 2002, grew to $716 million for 2003, and hit $841 million in 2004.

In February of 2003, William Donaldson--the same Bill Donaldson who co-founded Donaldson, Lufkin & Jenrette in 1959--was sworn in as SEC chairman. Over his varied career, Donaldson served as a Marine Corps officer, founded DLJ, worked for Henry Kissinger in the Nixon Administration, headed Yale University's School of Management, started his own investment firm, piloted the New York Stock Exchange, and ran Aetna, the health insurance giant. But the task of transforming the SEC from a dispirited and mismanaged government bureaucracy into the respected securities police force it once was would prove the most difficult challenge of his career.

Donaldson's most significant contribution to the SEC has been the creation of a new division, the office of risk assessment. Shortly after joining the commission, Donaldson said he was frustrated by the reactive nature of the SEC's response to the issues it faced. Like a police force, SEC enforcement attorneys only arrived on the scene after a crime or a fraud had been committed. The goal of the risk assessment office will be to identify problem areas before they mushroom into full-blown disasters.

Competition

Eliot Spitzer, the attorney general of New York, embarassed the SEC by investigating the abusive stock research programs at Merrill Lynch, Citigroup and other Wall Street giants. William Galvin, the top securities regulator in Massachusetts, humiliated the commission by responding immediately to Peter Scannell's complaints about market-timing abuses at Putnam Investments.

Through their actions, Spitzer and Galvin spurred other state regulators to crack down on bad behavior in the securities markets. As a result, the SEC, which used to have a monopoly on the enforcement of the nation's securities laws, now has competition in each state. This new landscape could ultimately benefit the SEC more than any internal management programs: after all, there's nothing like competition and threat of embarassment to spur greater productivity in a bureaucracy.

The SEC is also benefiting from significant budget hikes granted to it by Congress. But Congress, like the economy, moves in cycles. When the stock market cratered, and accounting scams at Enron and WorldCom were exposed, lawmakers were outraged and demanded that the SEC do more to fight that fraud. But when the current period of accounting scandals recedes, and the trials of CEOs such as Ken Lay, Jeff Skilling, Bernie Ebbers and Richard Scrushy are over, beware of a relapse.

Will investors ever flock again to the stock market? Certainly. Will campaign contributions continue to flow like a mighty river from Wall Street's banks to Washington? Absolutely. And because those contributions keep coming, look for Congress' zero-tolerance policy toward corporate fraud to fade someday. And on that day, the last line of defense standing between Main Street investors and another wave of accounting frauds will be an underfunded, overworked, emasculated SEC.

Epilogue

The wave of accounting frauds that swept through the securities markets in recent years bears an eerie similarity to the savings and loan crisis of the 1980s.

The savings and loan debacle came about when a sudden rise in interest rates put many small thrifts in a financial squeeze: they were paying out interest at higher rates than what they were collecting from long-term mortgage loans they had made a decade earlier at dramatically lower rates. Congress responded to their plight by relaxing bank regulations, allowing the thrifts to loan money out for speculative real estate developments and other risky ventures.

At the same time, a federal law increased the size of bank deposits guaranteed by the U.S. government from $40,000 to $100,000. That insurance removed the one brake necessary to keep bank managers in line, creating a situation known in banking circles as a "moral hazard." Because these bank managers knew that the capital they were loaning out was backed by Uncle Sam, they were willing to abandon their normal conservatism and roll the dice with their customers' money. Not surprisingly, when the commercial real estate market went bust in places like Texas and California, many of these speculative loans ended in default, causing the banks to fail and ultimately resulting in a $500 billion bailout of the industry by the U.S. taxpayer.

Less than 20 years later, a plague of accounting frauds swept corporate America, costing investors more than $500 billion, and draining $7 trillion from the nation's stock markets. Like the savings and loan crisis, these accounting frauds flourished due to an unusual combination of perverted incentives, approved by Congress.

After the savings and loan crisis, new regulations were put in place to insure that such a disaster could never occur again. As a result of those new regulations, the banking industry emerged in the 1990s healthier and more robust than it had ever been.

Just as banks bounced back from the savings and loan debacle, the business of selling stocks to investors would likewise be expected to improve following passage of the Sarbanes-Oxley Act and the subsequent increases in funding for the Securities and Exchange Commission. But don't bet on it.

The re-election of President Bush in November of 2004 may have hinged on the public's concern about moral values at home and terrorism abroad, but a second Bush term could have a profound impact on the relationship between Wall Street and Main Street. One of the president's boldest proposals is to "privatize" part of the nation's social security system. Since the 1930s, most working Americans have paid a portion of their earnings into the government's social security plan. That fund provides a monthly pension for retirees.

But because members of the so-called baby-boom generation, born between 1946 and 1964, are expected to drain that fund when they retire, the Bush administration has argued that today's younger workers should have control over their own retirement funds and be allowed to invest those funds as they see fit. With clear Republican majorities in both houses of Congress, it's possible that the President's vision could become law.

While privatizing social security makes sense, at least on paper, the events of the last few years should serve as a warning. To function properly, the nation's stock markets depend on honesty in corporate America, integrity among Wall Street investment bankers, and vigorous enforcement of the nation's securities laws by the SEC.

If there's one lesson we've learned from Enron, WorldCom and the other accounting frauds, it's that honesty among managers can't be legislated by Congress. And while Citigroup, Merrill Lynch and J.P. Morgan Chase have promised to mend their ways, the willingness of those banks to help Enron disguise its financial condition shows that most bankers can't be trusted to watch out for the average investor.

Finally, Congress opened its pursestrings in 2002 to increase the SEC's funding. But the increase in SEC funding and the passage of Sarbanes-Oxley came about only because voters were angry with accounting fraud. For the first time in years, lawmakers feared the voters more than the lobbyists. "There was a time when there was a power out there stronger than money," says Lynn Turner, former chief accountant at the SEC. "You had 90 million Americans saying they were going to vote their 401(k) plans. But Americans tend to have a very short memory."

Turner says the acute crisis of confidence that followed the exposure of WorldCom's fraud is now over, and that many lawmakers are once again putting the interests of their biggest contributors over the interests of average investors. "It's the same thing we went through in the 1990s," he says. "Because you've got very powerful, ongoing lobbying efforts with dollars backing them up, those interests overwhelm any notion of an obligation to investors. Investors will always come out second fiddle when Congress comes out to vote."

In order to prevent another accounting fraud crisis, one that could cripple the retirement savings of millions of Americans, Congress must ensure that the SEC is up to the task of policing the securities markets. To do that, lawmakers should consider the following changes:

• **The SEC should be self-funded.** Allow the SEC to keep the fees it collects from public companies. Self-funding would protect the financial health of the commission from the whims of its Congressional overlords, and allow the SEC to grow at the same rate as the financial markets it polices. When a city like Las Vegas explodes in size over a 10-year period, its police force grows accordingly. In the 1990s, Congress strangled the SEC in the midst of the greatest stock market boom in the country's history.

• **SEC attorneys should have criminal enforcement powers.** By itself, the SEC only has the power to bring civil suits against individuals and companies. As a result, many enforcement targets choose to fight the commission or enter into advantageous settlements in which they don't have to admit any wrongdoing. After the accounting frauds at Enron and WorldCom were exposed, the Department of Justice turned white-collar crime into a top priority. For the past few years, criminal prosecutors across the country have worked with the SEC to drive home the message that violating a securities law was as bad as robbing a bank. But interest in white-collar criminal cases will eventually wane, particularly outside New York, because those cases tend to be long and difficult to prosecute. If SEC attorneys could bring criminal charges on their own, they would be able to enforce the law without hoping for help from the Justice Department.

• **Give bonuses to successful SEC attorneys.** Plaintiffs lawyers who bring cases against tobacco companies and asbestos manufacturers put years of effort into the cause because if they win, the financial payoff is astronomical. But an SEC lawyer has almost no incentive, outside of a future job offer from the private sector, to take on difficult cases where the commission is outgunned by a public company's army of lawyers. If the SEC could reward its attorneys with a bonus for a job well done--say, a check for $50,000--its lawyers would work a lot harder and act more boldly on behalf of investors.

A new era is approaching, in which more Americans than ever before will put their savings and retirement funds into the stock market. Don't we owe it to ourselves and our children to make sure that the police force that patrols Wall Street has enough manpower and ammunition to do its job?

Notes

Chapter 1:

Information about Sam Waksal's sale of ImClone stock comes from court documents. Details about Waksal's personal life, including his prominent position in Manhattan social circles, comes primarily from two articles: "The Wacky Dr. Waksal," by Frank DiGiacomo and Ian Blecher *(New York Observer,* April 22, 2002); and "Investigating ImClone," by Alex Prud'homme (*Vanity Fair,* June 2002).

Arthur Levitt, former chairman of the Securities and Exchange Commission, describes his battle with the U.S. Senate over the expensing of stock options in his book, *Take on the Street* (Pantheon Books, 2002).

The rise in CEO pay is described in detail in a Towers Perrin report issued in 2000.

Chapter 2:

Other journalists and several former Enron employees have written books describing the fraud at Enron in exquisite detail. In the interests of reaching a wider audience, I have limited myself to a general, bird's-eye view of the fraud there. But for those who want to know more about Enron, the two best books on the subject, to my mind, are:

The Smartest Guys in the Room, by Bethany McLean and Peter Elkind (Portfolio/Penguin, 2003, 452 pages); and *Power Failure*, by Mimi Swartz, with Sherron Watkins (Doubleday, 2003, 362 pages). The first book is a thorough history of Enron's rise and fall, with vivid portraits of the main players in the drama, by two writers for *Fortune* magazine. The second tells the story of Enron's fall through the eyes of Sherron Watkins, the famed Enron whistleblower whose warnings of accounting trickery were largely ignored by chairman Ken Lay.

In addition to these books, *The Washington Post* published a penetrating five-part series of articles tracing Enron's collapse, called "The Fall of Enron," by Peter Behr and April Witt, from July 28, 2002 to Aug. 1, 2002. I relied on that series for the estimate of Enron's actual earnings for the year 2000, as well as for other threads of the Enron saga.

Reporters from *The Wall Street Journal* covered the unraveling of Enron doggedly. Where appropriate, I have credited that newspaper directly in the text.

Details of Rick Causey's conversation with Merrill Lynch bankers comes from court documents.

Information about the special purpose entities created by former chief financial officer Andy Fastow comes from court documents, as well as The Powers Report, a special report prepared for Enron's board of directors by a team of lawyers from the firm Wilmer, Cutler & Pickering.

Details concerning Enron's banking relationships with Citibank and J.P. Morgan Chase come from court documents, as well an investigation conducted by the U.S. Senate.

Chapter 3:

For the two major storylines of this chapter--the history of Arthur Andersen and the history of the accounting profession in the U.S.

since 1950--I relied on two books: *Final Accounting, Ambition, Greed & the Fall of Arthur Andersen,* by Barbara Ley Toffler (Broadway Books, 2003, 254 pages); and *Unaccountable: How the Accounting Profession Forfeited a Public Trust,* by Mike Brewster (Wiley, 2003, 297 pages).

Also of interest: a four-part series published by *The Chicago Tribune* on the decline of Arthur Andersen, which ran from Sept. 1, 2002, to Sept. 4, 2002, by Delroy Alexander, Greg Burns, Robert Manor, Flynn McRoberts and E.A. Torriero.

Chapter 4:

The vast majority of information concerning the accounting fraud at WorldCom comes from two internal reports. The first, an investigation ordered by Richard Breeden, a former SEC chairman appointed corporate monitor of WorldCom, was conducted by the law firm Wilmer, Cutler & Pickering. A second investigation was conducted by former Attorney General Dick Thornburgh, who was named bankruptcy court examiner after WorldCom filed for Chapter 11 bankruptcy protection from its creditors.

Details concerning Ebbers' personal life and spending habits come primarily from an article by two *USA Today* colleagues, Jayne O'Donnell and Andrew Backover, published on Dec. 12, 2002.

Although the story of how Cynthia Cooper unraveled the fraud at WorldCom appears in the Breeden and Thornburgh reports, it was first described in an article from *The Wall Street Journal* on Oct. 30, 2002. That article, by Susan Pulliam and Deborah Solomon, tells of the heroic actions Cooper and two subordinates took to get to the bottom of WorldCom's fictitious numbers.

Chapter 5:

Court documents filed by the Manhattan District Attorney's office detail Dennis Kozlowski's spending habits. But for a better picture of him, see two articles from *BusinessWeek,* "The Most Aggressive

CEO" (May 28, 2001), and "The Rise and Fall of Dennis Kozlowski," (Dec. 23, 2002). Also of note, from *The New Yorker*, "Spend! Spend! Spend! Where did Tyco's money go?" by James B. Stewart (Feb. 17, 2003). Mark Maremont and Laurie Cohen of *The Wall Street Journal* were the first to describe the Sardinian birthday party as well as the decorations in Kozlowski's luxury Manhattan apartment in an article published on Aug. 7, 2002.

Chapter 6:

Bill Owens' recording of his conversations with Richard Scrushy first became public in April of 2003. Court documents, including the U.S. Attorney's indictment of Scrushy, and several of the guilty pleadings by former HealthSouth financial officers, describe the nature of the alleged fraud. Much of the historical detail of Scrushy's creation of HealthSouth comes from articles in *Fortune, The Birmingham News* and *The New York Times*.

Chapter 7:

Historical information regarding the growth of stock research comes from articles in *Institutional Investor*. Details about Jack Grubman's correspondence with Sandy Weill and Henry Blodget's emails come from legal documents filed by New York State Attorney General Eliot Spitzer.

Chapter 8:

The assault on Peter Scannell was described by Jayne O'Donnell in *USA Today*, Nov. 20, 2003. Historical information about underfunding of the SEC has been detailed by various government reports, most notably a study by the General Accounting Office.

Special Thanks

This book would not have been possible without the invaluable support and contributions of the following: my wife, Cathy Taylor, who encouraged me every step of the way and sacrificed so much of her time in order for me to be able to write; my parents, David and Dorothy Farrell, who instilled in me a belief that journalism could expose and eradicate corruption; Mary Callahan, whose expert editing skills helped me focus and sharpen these chapters; Lynn Turner, the former chief accountant of the Securities and Exchange Commission, who served as an informal tutor to me when I started covering the SEC and acted as a sounding board for me on all matters involving accounting; Tracey Aronson and John Nester of the SEC, who helped me understand the commission's historical role in policing the nation's securities markets; Sherron Watkins, the brave Enron whistleblower who made herself available whenever I needed her expertise; Peggy Peterson of the House of Representatives' Financial Services Committee, who helped guide me through the halls of Congress; and my editors at *USA Today*, John Hillkirk, Jim Henderson, David Craig and Doug Carroll, who gave me the opportunity to cover white-collar crime and backed this project enthusiastically.

Finally, a tip of the hat to the wizard himself, Roy Williams, who got me to look up from the pile of documents I was buried in, and see the big picture. It was Roy's idea for me to write a book describing the accounting frauds of the past few years, and his inspiration that got me to turn that dream into reality.

What is Wizard Academy?

Composed of a fascinating series of workshops led by some of the most accomplished instructors in America, Wizard Academy is a progressive new kind of business and communications school whose stated objective is to improve the creative thinking and communication skills of sales professionals, internet professionals, business owners, educators, ad writers, ministers, authors, inventors, journalists and CEOs.

Graduates participate in online discussions and contribute to the weekly newsletters, monthly musepapers and books published by Wizard Academy Press.

Founded in 1999, the Academy has exploded into a worldwide phenomenon with an impressive fraternity of alumni who are rapidly forming an important worldwide network of business relationships.

"Alice in Wonderland on steroids! I wish Roy Williams had been my very first college professor. If he had been, everything I learned after that would have made a lot more sense and been a lot more useful... Astounding stuff."

- Dr. Larry McCleary,
Neurologist and Theoretical Physicist

"...Valuable, helpful, insightful, and thought provoking. We're recommending it to everyone we see."

- Jan Nations and Sterling Tarrant,
senior managers, Focus on the Family

"Be prepared to take a wild, three-ring-circus journey into the creative recesses of the brain...[that] will change your approach to managing and marketing your business forever. For anyone who must think critically or write creatively on the job, the Wizard Academy is a must."

- Dr. Kevin Ryan,
Pres., The Executive Writer

"Even with all I knew, I was not fully prepared for the experience I had at the Academy... Who else but a wizard can make sense of so many divergent ideas? I highly recommend it."

-Mark Huffman,
Advertising Production Manager, Procter & Gamble

"A life-altering 72 hours."

-Jim Rubart

**To learn more about Wizard Academy,
visit www.WizardAcademy.com
or call the academy at (800) 425-4769**

Index